Passionate
PRESENCE

Passionate
PRESENCE

*Experiencing the
Seven Qualities of
Awakened Awareness*

CATHERINE INGRAM

GOTHAM BOOKS

GOTHAM BOOKS
Published by the Penguin Group
Penguin Putnam Inc.,
375 Hudson Street, New York, New York 10014, U.S.A.
Penguin Books Ltd,
80 Strand, London WC2R 0RL, England
Penguin Books Australia Ltd,
250 Camberwell Road, Camberwell, Victoria 3124, Australia
Penguin Books Canada Ltd,
10 Alcorn Avenue, Toronto, Ontario, Canada M4V 3B2
Penguin Books (N.Z.) Ltd,
182–190 Wairau Road, Auckland 10, New Zealand

Penguin Books Ltd, Registered Offices:
Harmondsworth, Middlesex, England

Published by Gotham Books, a member of Penguin Putnam Inc.

First printing, February 2003
1   3   5   7   9   10   8   6   4   2

Lyrics from "Please Forgive Me" used by permission from David Grey.
David Byrne song titles used by permission from David Byrne / Index Music.
Lyrics from "Boogie Street" and "Waiting for the Miracle" used by permission
from Leonard Cohen.
Lyrics from Bob Dylan's "You're A Big Girl Now" Copyright © 1974, 1975 by
Ram's Horn Music. All rights reserved. International copyright secured.
Reprinted by permission.
Lyrics from "All I Have To Do Is Dream" written by Boudleaux Bryant,
© 1958 by House of Bryant Publications, renewed 1986.
Translated excerpts of Rumi © Coleman Barks, used by permission.
Poetry by Daniel Ladinsky used by permission.

Gotham Books and the skyscraper logo are trademarks of
Penguin Putnam, Inc.

LIBRARY OF CONGRESS CATALOGING-IN-PUBLICATION DATA
Ingram, Catherine, 1952–
Passionate presence : experiencing the seven qualities of
awakened awareness / Catherine Ingram.
p.   cm.
ISBN 1-59240-002-7 (alk. paper)
1. Spiritual life.   2. Awareness—Religious aspects.   I. Title.
BL629.5.A82 I54   2003
291.4'4—dc21   2002026076

Printed in the United States of America
Set in Granjon
Designed by Sabrina Bowers

To my brother Glenn Ingram
(1963–2002)
For Love

Contents

contents

acknowledgments

My life and work rely on a network of supporters that has allowed me the time to write this book while running an organization that services an international community. To each of those people, I offer my sincere gratitude. However, I would like to specifically express appreciation to those who have had a direct hand or eye on this manuscript or who have helped with its publication.

I am deeply grateful to my fantastic agent, Anne Edelstein, who has been a clear and steady voice throughout and whose values and priorities are impeccable; and to Lauren Marino, my wonderful editor at Gotham Books, whose enthusiasm, gentle persistence, and clarity elicited the most pertinent of the material. I am also grateful to Brooke Capps at Gotham Books for innumerable kindnesses and help in the production phase of the book.

I offer my sincere gratitude to my friends and colleagues who read all or part of the manuscript and who offered editorial suggestions or advice: Ron Alexander, Martha Bardach, Brandon Bays, David Berman, Andrew Beath, Ann Buck (and to Ann especially for providing writing refuge by the sea), Bob Chartoff, Leonard Cohen, Richard Cohen (and to Richard for his laser eye in editing), Julie Donovan, Jeff Gauthier, Hanuman Golden (and to Hanuman for years of encouragement to write a book), Alexa Hatton, Jim Hurley, my brother Bob Ingram, Arthur Jeon, Helena Kriel, Mick Marineau, Mignon McCarthy, Geneen Roth, Steven and Merlyn Ruddell, Bob Wisdom, and Michael Worle.

My overwhelming appreciation goes to my friends who helped shape some of the most important concepts of the book: the young geniuses in my life, Sam Harris in Los Angeles and Diarmuid O'Conghaile in Dublin; my longtime and wise assistant, Maria Monroe in Portland; and my sparkling muse for the allegory, Mimi Buckley in San Francisco.

I offer my heartfelt thanks to those friends whose guidance in various aspects of publishing was most helpful: Lama Surya Das, Mark Epstein, Tara Goleman, Mark Matousek, and Sharon Salzberg.

And lastly, I wish to express my humble gratitude to all those who call me *teacher* for all that they have taught me.

introduction

Over the millennia the search for meaning and belonging has been humankind's most fervent pursuit, and to that end religions and philosophies abound. Yet, in our time, many people feel alienated from all religion and philosophy, sensing them to be based in superstition, dogma, or hierarchies of power. The need for meaning and belonging remains the same, yet the traditional options for fulfilling that need have less and less appeal. In desperation, we have turned to consumerism, technology, and celebrity voyeurism as our new religions, and these, too, have proven unsatisfying. The modern world, for many, has become a soulless place.

Out of this disappointment comes a large and growing interest in finding meaning that is not based in beliefs or traditions, but instead relies purely on direct experience. Many people sense the spiritual, the mysterious breath of existence. Yet, though they sense the mysterious, they remain grounded in reason. Rational mystics, I call them. It may seem to such people that they are alone in their view, that they are not fit for either religion or the marketplace. They may feel that they are not fit for this world at all.

I know well the loneliness that comes when one no longer feels part of a spiritual tradition yet is wary of a purely mechanistic or biologically determined view of life. Some years ago I experienced an existential depression that lasted several years and fostered a cynical view of reality. Having previously been on a spiritual journey since the early seventies, I had studied with renowned teachers in Asia and the West and had immersed myself in a worldwide community of meditation practitioners, primarily in the Buddhist traditions. In addition to rigorous meditation practice, we studied what in Sanskrit is called the *dharma*, which loosely translates as "truth" or "the way." For over a decade I had also worked as a journalist specializing in consciousness and activism in order to have access to and, in a sense, private tutorials with some of the great spiritual leaders and thinkers of our time. These were heady years of feeling part of a growing spiritual movement.

But there came a point when none of it made sense anymore. All religious beliefs began to fall away and seem nothing more than fairy tales attempting to assuage anxiety about the purposelessness of existence and the fear of death. This falling away of beliefs occurred completely on its own and was the last thing I would have wished. After all, it is very comforting to have a nice coherent story about the purpose of life and a belief in the hereafter. Instead, I plummeted into a vision of reality that was pointless and heartless. Having long since seen the futility of finding peace in the pursuit of power or money, and, now, set adrift from any connection to dharma, I felt a stranger to every world. I no longer spoke the language of my oldest and dearest friends, and a cold desolation engulfed me.

The silver lining of the cloud of depression is that it sometimes opens us to fresh perspective. When our strategies have failed and we have found no consolation in any quarter, we can either fall into madness or into realizing that what we have always wanted—a passionate aliveness at peace in itself—is, strangely enough, found in a simple shift in perception.

In my case, meeting my teacher, the late H. W. L. Poonjaji of India, awoke in me a clarity that objectively viewed the story of my depression and pierced through it to underlying peace, dissolving the depression along the way. Poonjaji exhibited a possibility of living in the quiet center of one's being while remaining fully engaged in activity. His was a passionate expression of life, devouring its delights while remaining aware of its tragedies. Nevertheless, one sensed in him a silence that the world did not touch.

Despite my many years of meditation practice, I had never experienced silence in an ongoing way. I had tried to come to silence through techniques of taming the mind, and that had been futile. Yet now all effort to still the mind fell away and my attention began to effortlessly rest in the silence beyond thought. Crazy thoughts continued, but interest in them lessened. Movements of mind, emotion, fear, or elation became as waves on an ocean of peace. An acclimatizing process began to occur on its own. Just as mountain climbers, when approaching a high altitude, must spend time camped at points along the way with no particular task other than to let their bodies adjust to the new altitude, I could feel my awareness adjusting to silence while doing nothing to assist it. The silence did all the work, just as being at the higher altitude does the acclimatizing work for the climbers.

Within this silence, I also began to feel a pervading presence in everything, and a feeling of love overwhelmed me. I realized that I had always felt intrinsic presence and love on the periphery of my awareness; it was completely familiar. Pure presence is our fundamental experience, even when we seem to be lost in the stories and activities of life. Like breathing, it is taken for granted. Yet it is what we most clearly remember when we think back to the earliest times of our existence. The details of our past may be fuzzy, but *being* itself is clear. At the ages of four, ten, twenty, or ninety, what has or will most consistently define our experience is the simple fact of being and, if we go deeper, a feeling of love.

I remembered this feeling from my earliest days with my Italian grandmother, Caterina Versace, who died when I was seven and who had been like a mother to me. We would silently walk among the blue hydrangeas in her yard, and everything inside and out appeared to be glowing and shimmering. This all seemed perfectly normal at the time.

But, as I grew older, I somehow lost the sense of it. Although the awareness of simple presence and love was there all along, I overlooked it by searching for *meaning* and *purpose* and promises of life ever after. On meeting Poonjaji, the search fell away and in its place an appreciation for mystery and an awakened awareness emerged. I was overcome by the sensation of underlying unity. Everything was in its place—just so.

This understanding conveys a sense of belonging. I recognized that we are not merely interconnected; we are suffused with the same essence as that of everything. Steeping in this sense, we no longer spend our time clutching to what is turning to dust or chasing abstract ideas, such as *meaning* and *purpose*. We walk in a sense of totality; the world being entirely our own. It is not that we possess it but that we are it. Like water into water.

There is a story about a little fish who swims up to his older and wiser fish friend and says, "You go on and on about water. I have been searching for it everywhere and it is nowhere to be found. I have studied all the texts, practiced and trained diligently, and met with those who have known it, but it has eluded me." The wise old fish says, "Yes, dear. As I always tell you, not only are you swimming in it right now but you are also composed of it." The little fish shakes his head in frustration and swims away, saying, "Maybe someday I will find it."

We are so like the little fish. We search everywhere outside ourselves to try to find ourselves. We collect experiences, relationships, knowledge, and objects. We hope for recognition from others to validate our importance. But while we may have found pleasure or rewards in various ways, we have often overlooked our greatest gift, hidden in plain sight—our own passionate presence. We overlook this gift because we are so busy searching elsewhere for something more. As long as we depend on an enhanced sense of ourselves to be happy we are likely to be disappointed. Telling ourselves stories about what is missing forces us into a relentless pursuit of desires akin, as Poonjaji would say, to beasts of burden driven by a madman. Happiness comes in relaxed simplicity, living in present awareness, and contentment with this life that is granted.

Because it is simply what is so, this view comes effortlessly in deep relaxation. When striving is exhausted (usually through disappointment) and we no longer hope for anything outside ourselves to make us feel whole, we may begin to notice a startling quality of aliveness—how fulfilling it is just to be—and this sense of being infinitely extends and includes all of existence.

Usually people associate a sense of unbounded presence with epiphanies in life—being present at a birth, or a death. People lose themselves in sexual union, in nature, or in the presence of heart-wrenching beauty. In those moments they forget to keep up the story about the one having an experience, and all that is left is the actual experience of presence. Yet peak experiences are only portals to our true nature, which is already occurring completely on its own.

What is known as realization is merely feeling this immaculate presence here and now, realizing or being fully cognizant of the ordinary miracle of just being. This needs no attainment since it is already occurring. It requires no special circumstances, no life epiphanies, no meritorious preparations. It is fully present each moment of our lives. It stays fresh and innocent despite our sorrows, regrets, and whatever damage or failures we feel we have sustained. No suffering or transgressions have marred it, just as no exalted deeds have enhanced it. Countless thoughts and experiences have come and gone, and none of them have adhered.

Though meeting a teacher facilitated this awakening for me, it is not always necessary. In fact, awakened awareness is not dependent on any particular circumstance. We are each endowed with clear perception that becomes dormant or obscured through the conditioning of fear, loss, and belief. When we deeply relax in silence, our awareness effortlessly shines with a transforming brilliance. We live as sensible and practical people, but with a twinkle in our eyes. We go about our business as usual—answering phones, taking care of children, riding the subway—and we enjoy a quiet sense of presence through it all. Aware that we are living in a grand mystery, feeling the radiance of its presence everywhere, we also take care of the tasks at hand.

I began sharing these understandings in 1992, initially at the invitation of Ram Dass, spiritual teacher and author of the classic *Be Here Now*. Since that time I have traveled extensively, conducting public evening events in the U.S. and Europe. These gatherings, called Dharma Dialogues, are interactive discussions alternating with periods of quiet. The dialogue's purpose is to bring one's attention to present awareness and see through the mind's habitual ways of trying to squirm out of it. Each night is different, a kind of improvisational Socratic conversation that eventually leads, in almost each case, to silence.

In addition to Dharma Dialogues, I have also led many silent residential retreats. It is in the retreats, when people are simply quiet and free to float in the deep waters of their being, that I have noticed the emergence of a surprisingly consistent intelligence. This intelligence is cross-cultural and transcends biological abilities and educational back-grounds. People who may not have been considered intel-lectually gifted experience this intelligence as do people who have had little education. It could be thought of as an intelligence of the heart because it seeks harmony and the equilibrium of goodness. I call it *awakened awareness* be-cause it is innate and suddenly just wakes up. It is this awareness or intelligence we refer to when we say we are in our "right minds." We might add that awakened awareness is when we are in our right hearts as well. When we are in our right minds and hearts, we are instinctively loving, gen-erous, and clear.

For years I had been reflecting on the universal nature of this awareness. I had noticed, especially in retreats, that people in the daily group sessions would speak in almost mystical poetry to describe the ordinary events of their days. I realized that what we now call mystical works of poetry from former eras were simply descriptions of reality by people of those times, such as Rumi or Hafiz of the thir-teenth and fourteenth centuries. They weren't trying to be poetic. They were describing feelings and life as they liter-ally experienced them. They were reporting from the field of awakened awareness.

In retreat, I began to notice similar descriptions spoken by people who had never been exposed to these ideas. I have often been startled to hear perceptions and feelings de-scribed in nearly exact language by, for example, a person who lives in rural Scotland and one who lives in Hawaii. I realized that this intelligence crosses time as well, that the awakened awareness of the Buddha, Christ, or Rumi is not distinctly different from that of our own. People over the centuries have stumbled upon this inherent intelligence in countless ways and expressed it in art, poetry, music, science, and even religion.

My attention began to reflect on and marvel at the similar expressions I observed in people who exhibited awakened awareness. It became a secret hobby of mine to notice these similarities wherever I traveled in the world. One night I awoke from a dream in which I had identified seven primary qualities that naturally and consistently emerge in awakened awareness. I got out of bed, wrote them down, and went back to sleep. The next morning I looked at what I had written and saw the basis for this book.

The seven qualities—Silence, Tenderness, Embodiment, Genuineness, Discernment, Delight, and Wonder—are familiar to everyone. Yet we often overlook them in our pursuit of worldly things or spiritual advancement. In awakened awareness, however, these qualities are our daily company, our best friends. They come from our own innate wisdom and guide us better than any philosophy ever has.

This book is therefore simply a reminder of what you already know in your heart of hearts, in your own awakened awareness. Someone who recently read the manuscript said that during the reading she often found herself thinking,

"Yes, absolutely right, but how do we get there?" The irony is that in the moment of saying, "Yes, absolutely right . . ." she was in awakened awareness itself. It is your own awakened awareness that recognizes truth. You don't have to strain to find it or strive to intellectually hold onto it. Insight is best metabolized fresh. There is no need to remember anything for later. If you try to grasp it, you end up with dogma. If you relax into the quiet center of your being, your own awareness will notice every wink of the mystery that comes your way.

Passionate
PRESENCE

silence

She had been on the quest for so long that the reasons for it were no longer clear to her. She was just moving, step after step, too tired to think. Having recently fallen down a slippery bank into a thicket, she was bruised and scratched, her daring leaps of former times now too difficult to execute.

Seeing a river in the distance, she made her way there to get a drink and wash her wounds. Afterward she lay under a nearby tree thinking that if she could just get some rest, she would be able to renew her journey with invigorated determination. After all, the quest was important. The quest was all there was.

She was about to drift off to sleep when she noticed an old woman sitting on the riverbank nearby. The woman, who had been gazing at the water, turned and silently gestured to her, opening her arms with palms outward as if to say, "Just this."

Yes, just this, the woman thought as she fell into a deep sleep.

When she awoke several hours later, evening had fallen and the old woman was gone. Getting up, she realized that something was very different. The stars were now shining pinpoints within her being, their light no longer traveling from a distance but encompassed by her awareness as glowing prisms within the vast regions of herself. The river and its sound, the trees and their smell—all now existed in a sweeping whole, a multidimensional canvas of color, forms, and sensations. She realized in a flash that it had always been so.

Her restless thoughts, so long her only companions, disappeared into a void as soon as they arose, as though pulled into space. They were whispers in a cathedral. They were ghosts, without relevance. She remembered that she had been on a quest, but now the idea of it seemed strange, and she could no longer hold the thought of its importance.

The silence, on the other hand, seemed almost loud in contrast. She spent the rest of the night feeling like a bird that had been freed from a cage into a palace of starlight, the silence now and again punctuated by the words "just this," though even these words were claimed by it.

call off the search

"If you begin to understand what you are without trying to change it, then what you are undergoes a transformation."

—J. KRISHNAMURTI

My life as a seeker was motivated by a combination of suffering and a desire to feel passionately alive. With these motivations, I chased experiences, running away from my suffering self and running toward some imagined excitement. I wanted to see the range of possibilities wherein life's secrets might be hidden, and this resulted in an exhaustive pursuit.

As a spiritual seeker and journalist I sought out those whom I considered to be the wisest people of our time and interviewed many of them for publication over two decades. I helped organize meditation retreats and centers, alternative educational programs, an organization to represent dispossessed nations and peoples—and somewhere or other I met almost every person in those fields whom I had admired from afar or who I thought had something to teach me. I also explored a wide range of social strata, moving among the wealthy elite and among those on the impoverished fringe.

And I meditated. I watched my thoughts, sensations, intentions, itches, emotions, pain, and breath until I came to know the landscape of my mind so well that no madness in it could surprise me. For nearly twenty years I practiced Buddhist meditation in the U.S., Europe, and Asia, while studying the great texts of Asian philosophy.

I traveled the world many times over, sometimes as a dharma bum, sometimes as a bohemian journalist, and sometimes first class. I backpacked overland from Italy to India, hitchhiked across the Moroccan desert, swam with dolphins, kayaked with orca whales, slept under stars in Afghanistan, and hiked mountains in Argentina, Switzerland, and India. I drove on roads laden with land mines on the Cambodian border while reporting on the war there, and I sat with many of the great contemporary spiritual teachers in some of the most peaceful places on earth. I went to Ladakh the first year it opened for visitors, spent many nights watching bodies burn on river ghats in India, chanted to Siva till dawn in Benares, danced to reggae till dawn in Jamaica.

I watched lunar eclipses from a sailboat in the South Pacific while stoned on psychedelics and from the snowy grounds of a New England monastery while stoned on silence. I had an international community of interesting, funny, and kindhearted friends engaged in spiritual, social, and environmental causes. I attended conferences and vacationed in the world's most exotic playgrounds. I read important works of literature, nonfiction, and the new sciences. Along the way, I also had a number of romantic relationships with incredible men and once fell so wildly, passionately, and erotically in love that I may never quite recover from it.

But there was always something missing, and so the search went on. The problem was that no matter how satiated and alive I felt in moments of profound experience, it didn't last. Like the hunger that returns only hours after the gourmet meal, or the thirst that follows soon after being quenched, the experience of fulfillment was limited by time. I yearned for a satisfaction deep in my being, unmitigated by time, but I found only a collection of experiences that had all ended.

The search had been an attempt to make more of myself. No matter how noble my various endeavors, the intention to enhance *me* remained a primary motivation. Even in meditation practice there was a hope that I would attain something one day, something more would be added on. I would get the insight, realization, satori, or enlightenment, and then I might finally be able to relax. I was always toppling forward, looking for the next experience, the next fix. During an electrifying moment of aliveness, I would also be aware of its impending end and of the need to re-create the feeling again somehow. I would be distracted from the full enjoyment of it by a desire to savor it later. I would miss the experience I was having in the present, like people who go on adventures and spend most of their time taking photographs, trying to capture their moments for later enjoyment and seeing present reality only through a tiny lens, fixated on a future that never comes.

Meeting my teacher Poonjaji woke an intelligence in me that knew there was nothing to do or to get and that the search itself was the problem. The very idea of a search must begin by thinking that something is missing. It assumes deprivation at the outset. What if we knew that nothing is missing—right now—that nothing is needed for our experience of aliveness but being alive? What need would there be for a search? What would you hope for? Picture it right now. What do you want in the future? What would it give you if you had it? Whatever that is, is it not available right now in your own being? Poonjaji used to say that when you realize this you will burst out laughing because what you were looking for was always with you, hidden in plain sight. He likened this to "searching for one's glasses while wearing them."

In the deepest recesses of ourselves there is a most familiar quietude. It has been there through all our seeking and craving, as well as all the other events of our lives. It is a point of peace, a silent witnessing awareness that is fundamentally unperturbed no matter what happens. Steeping in this awareness, one is at ease in the present, fully welcoming what comes and fully releasing what goes—feeling alive throughout. This awareness is not something far away and in another time. It is already occurring right here and right now.

For instance, while watching a movie, we may swirl in a sea of emotions—fearful, romantic, humorous, or tragic. If the story is especially potent, we might feel all of these emotions in a single film. Yet no matter how swept away we might be by the movie or how gripped by the emotions of the experience, there is within us a quiet witnessing awareness that knows perfectly well that we are sitting in a theater all the while. If that were not so, we would surely flee the room as soon as any frightening situation occurred on the screen. We would run for our lives upon seeing the first weapon or firestorm coming at us, were it not for some part of our awareness knowing that the visions on the screen are not our most fundamental reality.

In a similar way, there is a field of silent awareness containing all the events of our days. Although we may sometimes be gripped by emotion or lost in a particular story, there is throughout each of our dramas a deeper reality of silent presence. This is a silence of the heart rather than an imposed cessation of speech or activity. It is a silence that is, we could say, the background of all activity. We don't need to find it because it is not lost.

If this is so, why is there so much searching and craving? Seeking is compelling because it produces a way for the mind to have a job. It seems that we are almost genetically programmed toward relentless mental occupation with desire and avoidance, a desperate squirming out of *now*. Perhaps nature has demanded that we keep on the move in order to stay alive, but this is becoming detrimental to life. We have evolutionarily outgrown the usefulness of being in a prevailing state of fear and greed in order to compete and survive. We can no longer afford it. It is driving us to disaster.

Nevertheless, it is strange how much we resist the inherent peace and quiet that is always possible. Perhaps this is because resting in simple presence is so foreign to a lifelong habit of mental complication, and we may have confused complication with a sense of aliveness. We might assume that having no particular mental project would result in boredom. Or we may be overwhelmed by how vast and free life suddenly feels when our minds are not on the hunt. As the prisoner who, upon being released, quickly finds a way to land himself back in jail, or the bird who resists the flight out when its cage door is opened, we are sometimes daunted by freedom and retreat into the cramped but familiar closet of a busy mind.

Yet in awakened awareness the mind acclimates itself to an expansion in silence. It gets used to letting neurotic thoughts drift and fade into nothingness, and it gradually loses interest in them even as they continue to arise. Disinterest in neurotic thoughts limits their power. What becomes more interesting is the open expanse of awareness through which all thoughts and everything else emerge and dissolve. And because this is ongoing, the perception of it can sneak up on you at any moment. Right now, as you read these words, you might sense the seamless field of presence in which you, the words, and all the things around you are floating.

This silent witnessing awareness brings with it a quality of brilliance, alert yet at ease. It is not the brilliance of thought but the brilliance of pure perception, an impersonal intelligence. It pays no particular attention to thoughts that would tempt it from its tranquility but doesn't mind that they come and go. There is no sense that something more is needed for contentment, and therefore a deep contentment prevails.

And suddenly the search is over. We have nowhere we need to go because all is in its place as is, ourselves included. We have nothing we need do to belong here because we feel no separation from existence. We still, more than ever, enjoy and passionately care about life, but we are no longer the beggar at its door, looking for love instead of being love. We realize that what we really wanted was not something that comes from seeking but that which comes from being found. We are as the prodigal son in Jesus' parable. After long wandering, being lost and depraved, and looking in all the wrong places for happiness, we finally come home. And just as the father embraced his wayward son and laid a feast in his honor, we are welcomed home into our own shining presence every time.

releasing the story

Even when there has been a strong recognition of presence, the habitual story about ourselves usually continues to arise. Our eyes open in the morning and at first we are simply aware of seeing and sensing. There is no thought of or reference to an entity having an experience. There is just pure awareness, simply being. Then slowly the thoughts begin to swirl and gather around the old well-worn subject, the story of "I." This story comes in as many versions as there are people to tell it. And the more it dominates the awareness, the more it demands to be told.

We all know the experience. We are cornered at a social event in which someone has launched into a long-winded listing of his accomplishments, his children and their accomplishments, his possessions, his opinions, his travels, what he likes, what he doesn't like, and what he plans to acquire in the future. We might feel that the man is barely aware of our existence except as a warm-blooded animal with the facility of hearing. And, in fact, we may be barely aware of him either. Our attention might be limited because a similar monologue about ourselves may be dominating our own awareness, though we might be restrained about vocalizing it.

It is called *the story,* and it is a way of thinking about oneself as a character who bases his inherent worth on acquiring things or experiences that make the character seem more interesting, successful, powerful, or sexy. The story may also be based on a character who sees himself as a victim and interprets events in the world to confirm his story of the hardship of life. His story may have more to do with all that he has suffered and now fears.

In both cases, the self-enhancing story and the self-denigrating story, the "I" character is always the star of the drama. We have rehearsed its lines and situations many thousands of times and are well practiced in our roles. We have imagined this entity for so long and with such intensity that the illusion, like any imaginary friend, seems to have a life of its own. Its adventures usually occur in one of two settings in time—past or future. And, of course, most of its future stories are simply based on pictures from its past. These stories may frighten, depress, or amuse us for a lifetime. Countless mental pictures of *me*—in the past, in the future, in the past, in the future.

As we walk through the landscape of the world, almost all that we see is interpreted with regard to its consequence to this character. The character of "I" is the central point of reference around which the story of the world revolves. I sometimes liken this self-referencing phenomenon to a metaphorical drama called *The Universe, Starring Me!*

When I was younger I had a great interest in my stories. I felt that the stories about who I was and what I had experienced needed to be frequently revisited as both a protection and a catharsis: a protection because I didn't want to make any of the worst mistakes again; and a catharsis because I felt that repeatedly telling the story would reveal what it all meant. I told my story to whoever would listen, until I had thoroughly bored all of my friends and eventually myself with it.

Now, it is not entirely inappropriate that one has a story with "I" as the central character. Having a strong sense of oneself, both psychologically and interpersonally, is a developmental necessity. The story of "I" begins very early in our lives, probably at around the age of two, at which point it revolves mostly around "I like" and "I don't like." This basic form of referring to the central character becomes more and more elaborate with time as the stories reflect more complicated desires and fears. Although the various events and emotions in the story develop dramatically throughout childhood and into adulthood (most of them now long forgotten), the idea of the central character remains the same, like the star of a long-running soap opera.

In awakened awareness, the story itself is not a problem.

It is perceived as a habit that has its place and function, but it no longer dominates awareness. Awakened awareness knows when aspects of the "I" story need to be addressed but otherwise pays little attention to them. It is primarily interested in the present, while the story is usually concerned with the past or future and is therefore released as it arises because awakened awareness recognizes how little of it is relevant. Simply through disinterest, the thoughts about the character called "I" arise and fade like bubbles in the sun. It doesn't matter that they continue to arise since they immediately fade away.

The fact is that all thought fades as soon as it arises. Of the millions of thoughts we have each experienced there is not a single one that has lasted. There are many that repeat in a similar way but each is actually distinct from previous ones. They all come and go in pristine awareness to which none of them adhere. There is no need to get rid of thought since there is no possibility of making it stay.

Being at home in present awareness was what my teacher called "keeping quiet." In this quiet he did not mean, "don't talk," "don't laugh," or even "don't shout." He referred instead to noticing the quiet that encompasses all activity, thought, and words. We simply experience *being* through breath, sensation, sight, sound, smell, or taste. These direct experiences require no reference back to an entity, nor do they need stories to enliven them. As this awareness becomes more our habit, self-referencing becomes tedious, an extra mental workload with no reward. Our awareness is then more interested in what we are experiencing in real time rather than in making up a story about an imaginary time with a leading role for *me*.

When we experience life directly, we are not chopping it up into distinct pieces or relying on pictures from the past to give it meaning. We are not even particularly interested in giving things meaning. We live in an innocence that accepts life as it comes without trying to appropriate every occurrence for a story or a myth.

This is not to suggest that there is no place for myths or stories. We communicate by telling our life stories, and our culture communicates by telling its myths. If one were to sit next to someone on a train, it would be offensive to say, "There is only the experience of this present reality" to their question, "Where are you from?" Likewise, in any interpersonal relationship there is the appropriate place for life stories. But we realize that telling our stories is really about connecting with, as Emerson put it, "that common heart of which all sincere conversation is the worship."

"That common heart" is found in silence. Just as silence is intrinsically the ground of all music, silence is also the ground of all stories. As the notes of a melody arise from and dissolve into silence, our stories arise from and dissolve into silence as well. In confusion, we pay attention mostly to the stories. In awakened awareness, we pay attention mostly to the silence.

beyond words

*"When you are deluded and full of doubt, even a thousand
books of scriptures are not enough. When you have realized,
even one word is too much."*

—FEN YANG

Years ago I was in India when the Shankaracharya, the
Hindu equivalent of a pope, died. *The Times of India* published a number of eulogies about the renowned master,
one of which was written by a well-known journalist and
friend of India's former prime minister Indira Gandhi. It
seems that Mrs. Gandhi would occasionally consult with
the Shankaracharya in moments of turmoil during her ad-
ministration as prime minister. On one visit to the holy man
she invited her journalist friend to go with her. They flew
by private plane, and upon arrival Mrs. Gandhi was immediately taken to see the Shankaracharya alone. After a couple hours she returned to the plane, and she and the
journalist headed home to New Delhi. The journalist noticed that a deep serenity had come over the prime minister,
and after some time he couldn't help but ask, "Mrs.
Gandhi, what happened in there?"

"It was wonderful," the prime minister replied. "I put all
my questions to him, and he answered every one of them,
but neither of us spoke a word."

The power of the Shankaracharya's presence was so strong that it awakened the prime minister's remembrance of her own. She found herself in the quiet understanding wherein questions are either answered or fade away. "The still small voice within" turns out to be silent. It perceives with an intelligence that has not been learned, an intelligence that is innate.

In awakened awareness we use language to communicate while knowing that another, more powerful communication is taking place in deeper awareness. Over the course of nearly thirty years I have been attending silent retreats, shared with literally thousands of people during that span of time. I once found myself in a remote part of the world where I ran into someone I had known from several retreats. Walking toward him with a smile on my face, I thought to myself, "Oh, there is my good friend . . . ," at which point I realized that, because we had always been silent together, I had never actually known his name. Nor had I known his nationality or his occupation. I knew nothing of his biography at all.

Yet I knew his being. I had seen him watching birds at sunset in the same spot each day. I had noticed the care with which he quietly removed his shoes before entering the meditation hall. I had been the recipient of his kindness when he helped me carry some of my belongings out of the rain. We had shared silent presence throughout the days and nights. Yet we had never once heard each other's stories. Our only communication had occurred in what singer/songwriter Van Morrison calls "the inarticulate speech of the heart."

In awakened awareness we need not pretend that we are only a conglomeration of stories, an aggregate of accomplishments, or a survivor of miseries. We are willing to gaze into the eyes of another without fear or desire—without stories about who I am or who she is—and sense there only the light of existence shining in a particular pair of eyes.

In retreats we also notice the power of words to condition perception. By naming things we invoke a preconceived picture of the object or event and we therefore have a conditioned response to it, if only momentarily. Now, of course, language is a fantastic communication tool, necessary and useful. But it is helpful to know its place in our awareness and the limits of its usefulness. I often say, in paraphrasing Shakespeare, "A rose by *no name at all* would smell as sweet." There is an awareness that exists beyond words and allows our direct experience to be completely fresh. The more attuned we are to this awareness, the more quickly language and thought are analyzed for their usefulness and released. This occurs by what I call "steeping in silence," whereby the attention rests in quiet awareness and remains there more and more consistently, becoming stronger in its habit.

I always bring a thermos of tea to Dharma Dialogues and sip the tea throughout the evening. Sometimes, I forget to rinse out the thermos until the next morning, and if there was any tea left, it will have become much stronger than it was the night before. There was no tea bag in the thermos overnight. Only the tea. It became stronger by steeping in *itself.* Like this, our awareness in quiet becomes stronger by steeping in itself.

This adaptation to silence also dissolves barriers between us. Although words are mainly intended to form bridges of communication, they often have the opposite effect. Many people use words simply to fill the quiet. They are uncomfortable with silence and so they chatter. They hope to connect with others, but often the chatter prevents any real communication. In awakened awareness, one recognizes in the chatter an attempt for contact. Underneath the babble is someone who wants to be accepted, understood, or loved. What is seen by clear awareness in such cases is the simplicity of being, the human warmth beneath the torrent of words. The words then become nothing more than a little static in an otherwise clear transmission. However, if both minds are full of static, there is little possibility for knowing each other in the place where two are one. On the other hand, if two minds are well steeped in silence, a fantastic communication ensues. Thich Nhat Hanh once said of his friendship with Martin Luther King, Jr., "You could tell him just a few things, and he understood the things you did not say."

I have several times been privileged to be in the company

of great teachers meeting each other for the first time. When I was younger I remember hoping that I would be privy to esoteric dharma discussions among the great ones or that they would perhaps dissect their philosophical differences and provoke a general debate among their students. But what usually happened was that they would just twinkle at each other. They would politely exchange pleasantries or discuss the weather, but mostly they were quiet, just twinkling away. Someone once asked the great Indian teacher Nisargadatta Maharaj, (whose dialogues in the classic book *I Am That* are some of the most powerful words on unbounded presence in print) what he thought might happen if he met Ramana Maharshi, another of the great saints of India. "Oh, we would probably be very happy," replied Nisargadatta Maharaj. "We may even exchange a few words."

the wellspring of genius

"*Silence is the element in which great things fashion themselves.*"

—THOMAS CARLYLE

Picture a single stroke of calligraphy on a white canvas. Every marking of ink by the brush stands out in full relief against the white background. Every nuance of the freedom in the stroke as it had once flowed and swept across the canvas is clearly visible. Now imagine the canvas full of random chaotic scrawls such that there is hardly a square inch unmarked. Imagine also that the same calligraphy is among the scrawls as well, but of course now it is much harder to see or even to find. As beautiful as it may have been, it goes unnoticed amid the chaos.

Just so, the strokes of genius in our minds. In silence our creative flickers of genius stand out in clear relief as soon as they arise. In chaotic mind, a mind obsessed with thought and neurosis, flickers of genius often go completely unnoticed. They may arise frequently, bursts of inspiration coming from some mysterious source, but if the mind is transfixed by its jumble of thoughts, the impulses of genius just flicker back into the void.

Now, some people think that great creativity comes from mental agony. They speculate that quietness of being is not useful for creativity, citing the lives of many great artists who were seemingly depressed or even suicidal. If we look at the life of Vincent van Gogh, for example, we might conclude that depression was conducive for producing great art. But I suggest a different interpretation for the source of his art. Perhaps it was only during the act of painting that he experienced the deep peace of simply being. When in the act of painting, Van Gogh may well have had a special connection, an exalted connection, to a sense of pure presence, and from that deep silence his fantastic paintings emerged. Painting was perhaps his doorway to the divine. The beauty he saw suggests an unclouded awareness, no matter the demons that haunted him at other times.

Mystics, mathematicians, poets, writers, and dreamers all tell us that their visions come to them seemingly out of the blue, when there is no trying to perform or impress. One may be walking in the garden, another taking a shower, another sitting quietly watching the rain when suddenly the insight or vision comes shooting like a comet through the sky of awareness. From where does this genius arise? It comes from the inherent intelligence that is available when we are quiet, when our minds are not running the show. It is upstream from thought. Awakened awareness.

The creativity that emerges from this kind of intelligence is different from that born of ambition. Ambition is generally driven by ego-based needs, thoughts of "I." With this motivation, the desire to create is mainly the desire to create a legend, a legend called "me." People erect towers of varying types of achievements and publicly dedicate them, but their internal dedication is to *I*. "I did this; I must be grand." The creativity that comes from ambition often has the taint of ego in it, no matter how majestic or laudable the production. Its contribution usually serves the general thrust of competition in the world. It titillates the movements of ego and often fosters jealousy and resentment.

The creativity that comes from silence, from a quiet heart, feels different from that of ambition to both the creator and the observer. When the artist or the worker is out of the way, both the creator and the observer experience the art as simply a gift, an expression of the impersonal intelligence shared by all. The creator has no need to take credit for it, the observer no need to possess it. Some of the most beautiful works of art on earth were created anonymously: most of the ancient Chinese paintings of the Ming dynasty, which influenced Asian art for the next thousand years; the great Buddha statues of Sri Lanka; the pyramids, which were built in Egypt when they had no words for *art* or *artists;* and many of the intricately patterned Amish quilts of the last two hundred years. These anonymous works speak to the quiet within each of us.

Sometime in the late 1970s, a friend and I visited an exhibit of Japanese landscape paintings on scrolls by Zen masters of the fifteenth century. Each scroll represented a small world of peace. They depicted lovely scenes of nature, temples, mountains, and monks pointing to the moon, surrounded by a preponderance of sky represented by white space. Walking through the exhibit, we became more and more quiet. It felt as though a cool breeze swept through my being, as though I were walking on ancient paths of peace. We had received a transmission of silence from the Zen masters in the form of their art, so powerful was the awakened awareness that had produced those paintings some five hundred years earlier.

As we left that exhibit, we passed through a section of the museum where European paintings from around the same time were displayed. Pictures of beheadings and gore abounded, usually attached to some religious symbolism. The characters in the scenes were ornately and heavily clothed. Surrounded by opulence, food, and drink, their general demeanor seemed miserable. Every inch of canvas was covered and all of it depressing. This, too, was a transmission. I felt the weight of living in that time and place where awakened perception was likely quashed or persecuted wherever it arose. Leaving aside the technical accomplishment of the paintings, I found the art from that period a transmission of gloom. I felt compassion for the people of that time along with gratitude for living in the time and place that I do.

The experience in the museum that day has informed my relationship to creative expression ever since. When viewing art through awakened awareness, one feels directly into the moment of its creation and clearly senses the heart of the artist. This transmission comes to us in printed words, sculptures, buildings, dances, movies, and children's coloring books. It comes to us anywhere that life articulates itself, and it crosses time.

Creative expression that flows through awakened

awareness penetrates the receiver in an unforgettable way. Consider the words that have come to us from Lao Tzu, Chuang Tzu, the Chinese Patriarchs, or the Buddha. Their words hold power after thousands of years because their very lives were the creative expression of universal intelligence, some of its most stunning works of art. We have forgotten the kings, the dancers, the politicians, and the painters of those times. But we have remembered the awakened ones; their presence lives as a reminder of the presence within each of us, a wellspring of genius that makes timeless art of our temporal lives.

aloneness

"In solitude we are the least alone."

—LORD BYRON

It is said that some of his students once asked Rumi to reconcile his incessant speaking on the subject of silence. Rumi replied, "That which is truest of me has never uttered a word."

There is a depth in each of us that has never uttered a word. It is a place of total aloneness. "A path so narrow," my teacher would say, "that two cannot walk abreast." No matter how connected with community, family, friends, society, or nature we might feel, there is a deep silent aloneness in us all. We know that the experiences we have had, the secret moments of joy, beauty, or love, as well as the particular shades of our sorrow, can be fully known only to ourselves. We may share events with others, but we are each on our own inner journeys, and each is completely unique. For this very reason—the singular expression that we each are—aloneness is inevitable. The creative force of the universe does not make exact copies, even in clones, so there is no escaping the aloneness that is part of being an original work of cosmic art.

And yet much of human activity aims at avoiding this very fact. People are often terrified of aloneness because they experience it as loneliness. They keep busy with work, stay in motion by traveling, or surround themselves with people at almost all times. They might use intoxicants, television, sex, or food to dull the awareness of deep aloneness. But it lurks in consciousness and sneaks up on them, cold and desolate, any time of the night or day. The efforts to avoid feelings of loneliness may actually cause the feelings to be more intense when they finally break through. We do what we can to distract ourselves from these feelings, but in our private moments they arise with a vengeance and with them a kind of madness. This madness can induce desperate and harmful actions. Much of the trouble in the world may simply be the result of resistance to our irrefutable aloneness. As the French philosopher Blaise Pascal noted in the seventeenth century, "All of man's miseries stem from his inability to sit quietly in a room and do nothing."

In awakened awareness the experience of aloneness is not a cause for fear or despair. It is a sanctuary of silence, a private abode, "a room of one's own"; the one place loneliness cannot reach. Aloneness in this sense is not a hardship of isolation but a refuge from the demands of constant mental and physical activity. When we know our aloneness in this way, we feel it even in the midst of activity. We feel it when we are with others or with that one special other. We feel it when on a podium speaking to hundreds of people or at a family gathering of dozens of relatives. As Albert Einstein wrote: "I am truly a 'lone traveler' and have never belonged to my country, my friends, or even my immediate family with my whole heart; in the face of all these ties, I have never lost a sense of distance and a need for solitude, feelings which increase with the years."

My teacher Poonjaji was as a lion in his aloneness. For many years he wandered in the foothills of India, sometimes sharing dharma with the few people who would chance upon him, sometimes traveling with another, but mostly walking alone and letting fate take him where it would. He kept diaries for some of that time, and reading them is an insight into awakened mind. He would often mark the date and place of a journal entry, but beyond that there would be nothing about the local area, people, or sights he had seen. His interest was in a journey occurring on another scale of time and space. A typical entry: "In me the universe moves hither and thither, impelled by the wind of its own inherent nature."

I met Poonjaji much later in his life. His health had diminished to the point that he could no longer walk without help, and consequently he was almost always surrounded by people. Yet I have never sensed anyone so alone. His was a majestic aloneness, like that of the ocean or the sky. For me his aloneness is probably the most inspiring aspect about him. He lived in a depth in which one can bring nothing and no one—no friends, no children, no spouses, no possessions.

In Dharma Dialogues I often refer to this majestic aloneness as "a mountain seat of freedom." It is as though one is resting on a mountaintop, quietly gazing into vastness, enjoying space in all directions. Welcoming whatever arises in the sky, one notices that thoughts pass by like clouds, feelings fade like rainbow colors, sensations flicker like birds twittering. Here is only the luminous present, the open expanse of being, and whatever is passing through the sky right now. A sense of fullness prevails. No attention is paid to mental commentary about what should or should not be happening. There is just relaxation into what is— only suchness.

And, finally, in awakened awareness aloneness becomes irrelevant. The sense of it fades as there is no one to feel alone, no one to speak about the majesty of aloneness. All mental activity effortlessly subsumes into the silence from which it arose. There is no feeling of self or other than self. There is only the wind blowing through boundless awareness, the light shining in our eyes, and the sounds of life reverberating right through us.

peace

"Lulled by Time's beats, eternity sleeps in us."

—SRI AUROBINDO

There is a fable about a young man who lived long ago in Istanbul, Turkey. Because he was poor, he had only a single room, sparsely furnished with a few books and a small cot for a bed. One night the young man had a dream—a vision, really. In it he saw himself walking on a street in what he came to realize was the city of Cairo in Egypt, a place he had never been. He could clearly see the name of the street and the houses that lined the road. In the vision he walked up to one particular house, noting the address. He entered into a tiled courtyard and then into the main house. An open door drew him to a particular room within the house. In this room sat an old man surrounded by treasures beyond anything the young man had ever imagined.

Diamonds, emeralds, and rubies were piled high in pyramid shapes. Gold and silver bars lined the walls. Exquisite carpets and artifacts from around the world lay at his feet. The young man stared at the treasures and then at the old man in amazement, for in that moment he somehow knew that these treasures belonged to him. He didn't know how he knew (it was a vision, after all) but he was certain that all of it was rightfully his.

The young man bolted awake from the dream. So confident was he in its veracity that he set off that very day on the long journey from Istanbul to Cairo in order to claim his treasure. In those days travel was slow and the young man, being poor, had to work along the way to pay for food and lodging. After several months he eventually arrived in Cairo. Upon making inquiries, he found the very street he had seen in his dream. As he set foot upon it, everything seemed completely familiar. The houses were exactly as he had seen them in his dream/vision. And sure enough, the house that in the dream had contained the old man and his treasure was precisely where the young man expected it to be. Knowing his way, he entered into the tiled courtyard and then into the room of treasures where he planned to make his claim.

There sat the old man, but there were no jewels, no gold or silver, no carpets or artifacts. The young man, undeterred by the absence of the treasures, recounted his vision to the old man and concluded by saying, "Since everything else in my vision has been accurate, I assume that the riches are hidden here somewhere. Please hand them over to me."

The old man was silent for some time, looking intently at the young man, his eyes glistening. After a while, he spoke. "It's strange," he said. "I, too, had a dream. I dreamed of a young man in Istanbul who looked exactly like you."

"Yes, go on," implored the young man, certain that this information would lead to his treasure.

The old man proceeded to describe the street on which the young man lived in Istanbul. He described the young man's mother and father, his siblings, his friends at work, and the books on the wall of his simple room. "In my vision," said the old man "the greatest treasure, more precious than all the shiny rocks and metals of the world, was there on a small cot in that room."

The young man suddenly realized what the old one meant. In that moment, he saw that his existence, his very being, was all the treasure he would ever want or need. A profound peace overcame him. He bowed to the wise man and, taking his leave, returned home to Istanbul where he lived out his quiet days.

While the young man's journey home to himself dominates this story, I am equally interested in the role of the old wise one. His presence and clarity were so strong that with just a few words from him the young man awoke to the greatest realization of his life. This story illustrates how the peace of simply being is not only a reward in itself but a blessing to all who encounter it. In it, one becomes as a large shade tree quietly offering comfort and shelter to those in the various storms of life.

In becoming refuges of peace, we have likely had to go through our own journeys of confusion, just like the young man in the story. This enables us to understand those who do not sense their own simple presence, searching everywhere else for it, like "the musk deer who searches the world over for the source of its own scent," as Ramakrishna said. Hoping to find something to make it all okay or to feel good about ourselves, we will try anything, and we often end up only making matters worse. Our hunger for finding treasures or any other circumstances that we think will bring us peace inhibits our resting in the peace that we are.

In awakened awareness there is no notion that peace is found anywhere but in one's being. Much of our world is in chaos and has been so for as long as we know. Even in times of relative peace the daily events of life can go haywire at any moment: trouble with a spouse, children, or friends; difficulties with one's job; loved one's having accidents or falling ill; one's own health becoming precarious; relatives and friends dying. When we read and listen to the news, this world can truly seem like hell. War, environmental devastation, starvation of millions, random violence, terrorism, torture, and children being kidnapped and murdered are reported daily with the steadiness of a drumbeat. How can any of us find peace in such a world? The answer is, we cannot. There is no lasting peace to be found in the circumstances of the world. If the humans don't get you, nature will.

And yet there is a sanctuary. It is not in the circumstances of the world but in the recognition of the silence that contains it. This silence is our own deep and true nature, and we can visit it or live in it any time we remember to do so. In Dharma Dialogues, people sometimes wonder what they can do for the world. I speak of the necessity of knowing the treasure of *being* itself and finding there the peace that is not dependent on anything else. This understanding brings calm to everyone who encounters it. It decreases the violence and fear in the world, and it reminds others of the gift that is more precious than all the riches ever known. In silence, we can feel it: eternity sleeping in us.

tenderness

Dawn came and she arose from her seat. Sun-

light and mist mingled on the river as she walked

along its bank without purpose or destination. In

previous times she would have been heading

toward something, going but not arriving. Now,

though she was in motion, she was not going

33

anywhere. She was only here, step by step, walking by a river.

After some time she saw them: two sets of footprints along the shore; one set made by little feet. Farther along the prints had washed away; gone without a trace. This is the nature of all things, she reflected; each footprint, creature, plant, rock, and galaxy on a course of becoming, disintegrating, and ceasing to exist. Everything dissolving in time, all subject to annihilation at any moment. She considered the poignancy of existence, the inevitability of love and loss. Her recognition, unsentimental yet tender, induced feelings of compassion for all that lived, all that had lived, all that would live. The beings of time.

Even now one of them caught her eye. A large beetle on the path had somehow toppled onto its back, its wriggling legs announcing its will to live and blending with her own. Without thought she swiftly responded. Gathering up two large leaves she carefully placed one on each side of the beetle and gently scooped it right side up. She watched it scurry to the safety of nearby foliage.

the dalai lama and the dog boy

Over twenty years ago, while staying in Bodh Gaya, India, my friends and I began hearing rumors about a boy who had allegedly been found among wild dogs. The rumor in town was that his seemingly canine behavior, lack of speech, inability to walk upright or to eat with his hands indicated that he had probably been raised among the dogs. We were intrigued. I had read *Gazelle Boy,* about a child who had been raised by gazelles in Africa, and I had also been fascinated by the story of "the wild boy of Aveyon" found in France in the 1800s. So it was with enthusiasm that I accepted an invitation to see the boy at a private gathering with the Dalai Lama, who had expressed an interest in the child. The meeting was to be held at the Gandhi Ashram where the boy was staying among a group of social workers and behavioral therapists who had assembled around him. A friend and I attended the meeting of about twenty people.

Judging from his size, the child appeared to be about five or six years old. Crawling on all fours, his eyes darting from side to side, he was like a frightened animal. Seeing him made me uneasy, such as when I have seen depictions of creatures that are half human and half some other animal. I felt a primal recoil from something alien. This surprised me because I had expected compassion to be my primary response to the boy.

The Dalai Lama was seated in the center of the room, and the child was brought before him. As the Indian officials and therapists began making their presentations about the boy to the Dalai Lama, he reached down and began to gently stroke the child's head, much as one would pat a dog. The gathered assembly pretended not to notice. Was it okay to treat the boy like a dog, or was that not good for his "rehabilitation"? The officials continued explaining their efforts to train the child to walk, to form words, and so on. All the while, the Dalai Lama continued to stroke the boy's head and shoulders, smiling and warmly murmuring until the child eventually curled up at his feet.

I could only imagine the comfort for that boy in those moments. Whatever his history had been, I was sure that his current circumstances in his new life with strange and powerful creatures must have been at least difficult and perhaps terrifying. Here, if only for a short while, one of the strange creatures met him—being to being—and communicated in his only shared language, the language of the heart.

Heart language has one thing in common the world over. It is the quiet offering of understanding to others without the demand for being understood oneself. Certainly, being understood is wonderful. It is delightful to be met in the deepest aspects of our being and a cause for celebration when it happens. But wishing to be understood by others, to be met in the deep places, often leads to disappointment. Understanding others, meeting them wherever their hearts reside, brings peace to oneself and has the greatest potential to transform difficult situations for others. No matter how seemingly great the gap in communication, most creatures respond to a loving presence. Almost all of us can feel when someone has our best interests at heart, listens with an open mind, and offers comfort without seeking benefit for himself.

In awakened awareness, a channel of communication easily opens because we don't need anything in particular from the other person. Real love doesn't seek to acquire. It gives itself away. Its very nature is that of surrender, service, and generosity. Just as galaxies gravitationally pull toward each other to explode in cosmic union, the force of love is such that it spends itself entirely. It gives away the store. And it does so for one simple reason; it cannot help it. It has no choice.

Many people feel this kind of helpless love only for their close relations. They have a few small concentric circles of dear ones for whom they feel varying degrees of consideration, but at the border of the outer circle, consideration comes to an abrupt halt. Everyone outside of this final circle is "other." From an evolutionary point of view, care for immediate relatives is part of the genetic imperative, a trait shared by most animals. But while that is natural and beautiful in its own way, there is a more expansive understanding of love and relatedness that transcends our biological dictates.

In awakened awareness, love is not tribal but universal. While we deeply honor family bonds and feel special connections to our community, we abandon the mentality of exclusion. No longer a slave to primitive impulses and irrational injustices based on race, ancestral, or even species affinities, we can see the bigger picture. After all, on a purely genetic level, all creatures have emerged from and share a river of DNA.

There is an even greater understanding which knows that what animates us is the animating force flowing through everything and is the purest expression of being. That is our true kinship, our great ancestor—the permeating universal force. Understanding this, everyone becomes family and every place, home. No matter how strange a given person or creature may be, we meet him in the understanding of our commonality. As psychologist Carl Jung once put it, "At times I feel as if I am spread out over the landscape and inside things, and am myself living in every tree, in the flashing of the waves, in the clouds and animals that come and go, in the procession of the seasons."

Some people may not want to risk feeling this kind of expansion. They may point out that the world is too dangerous to let down our guards and that it is foolish to be so open. While it is true that there are those who are dangerous to others and whom it is best to avoid if possible, there is an understanding in awakened awareness that stays open even in times of caution. It sees ignorance instead of evil in people who wish to harm others and is therefore not as frightened by them. In awakened awareness, we still get out of their way, but we do so as one might avoid an oncoming cyclone. We have no belief that says a particular person or being is an evil alien force. Though disturbed, he is still one of us.

Sensing nothing as alien to ourselves, we embrace the world as our own. Some aspects of it are wonderful and some are awful, but it is all familiar because its fundamental essence is the same. The homeless guy on the street corner who smells of urine, the confident businessman at the committee meeting, the angry woman pushing in line at the theater, the puppy sniffing every inch of ground it passes. In awakened awareness, they are each familiar, and we meet them in understanding, without the need to be understood.

loss and grief: doorways to empathy

"There is no coming to heaven with dry eyes."

—THOMAS FULLER

Last year I spent an afternoon at a cancer center in Los Angeles. I was waiting to see a highly regarded oncologist about a medical problem that, according to several doctors I had previously seen, might be malignant and require surgery. As it happened, the oncologist assured me that the condition was almost certainly benign and sent me home, suggesting no further treatment beyond "keeping an eye on it." Naturally, I felt the peculiar elation one feels with the experience of reprieve—a joy induced not by what happened but by what didn't happen. I thought of my friends and family who were waiting to hear the results of this visit and couldn't wait to share the good news with them.

As I left the doctor's office, I passed once more through the waiting room where I had spent an hour and a half observing other patients waiting their turn. Scarves, wigs, and gaunt faces signaled that many of these people had cancer. They and their loved ones had not heard good news following their visits to the doctor. They had been going about the usual business of their lives one day, and the next they were facing a struggle for their very existence.

I was again reminded of the universal nature of loss. I had dodged the bullet this time, but I knew that the reprieve was temporary. At any moment, everything could change. I looked around at the people in the waiting room and felt the precious commonality of being human—physically vulnerable, bonded with all that we love and enjoy, and due to be parted from every last bit of it.

The gift of this understanding is in the empathy it evokes. Each of us will know loss. Most of us have known a great deal of loss already. If we allow feelings of grief to be directly experienced in open awareness, these feelings call forth compassion for all who will suffer or have suffered loss.

Not only is this understanding a doorway to empathy, it is also an antidote to envy. We may see others who seem to have it all and feel that we lack in comparison. We should remember that if those who have great abundance are tightly clutching it, they have that much more to lose. Some people may suffer greatly from a loss that appears small while others bear lightly a loss that appears great. But in the end everyone will be parted from all they hold dear. As I often say in Dharma Dialogues, "*Samsara*[1] is not for sissies."

Sometimes people seem broken by what they have lost. We sense a prevailing bitterness and an emotional hardness as though they are bearing up, but with resentment toward life. Out of fear of experiencing any more loss people resolve never to love again. What they fail to see is that their resolution becomes their prison and, by resisting all potential for sadness, entirely shuts off the beauty of life as well. As Rumi said, "Gamble everything for love; halfheartedness does not reach into majesty."

To live in majesty is to live with a broken heart. If one isn't at least partially sad in witnessing this world, then one is not paying attention. What if we just let our hearts break over and over? Why not get used to living with a broken heart? In empathy with others we experience a vast range of human feelings. Their suffering is our suffering; their joys, ours. The degree to which we allow empathy with

---

1. Samsara: *Sanskrit. "The wheel of existence."*

sorrow is the exact degree to which we encompass joy. As Kahlil Gibran said in *The Prophet,* "Your joy is your sorrow unmasked."

In awakened awareness we are not afraid of intense feelings of either joy or sorrow. We know that these feelings are part of being alive and connected to all that live. We have no capacity for denial. We wear our tenderness on our sleeves, keeping company with the brokenhearted because they are the ones who meet in love.

Some of the most content people I have ever known are those who help others through loss and grief. This kind of work, though it has its share of sadness, invokes an intimacy that is not often found in any other context. The priorities become clear. What really matters after all? In the face of loss, the usual mental grousing about things of little consequence quiets down and the awareness is filled with a bigger picture, an appreciation of the immeasurable gift that is life.

In awakened awareness, we don't need to wait for the experience of loss to know what really matters. The awareness of loss and death lives gently in our consciousness as a reminder to fully live and love while we are here. It also provides a doorway of empathy for every other being. At the very least we will all share this final experience; we will all face death. Because we know how dear life is to most of us and the inevitability of its ending, empathy comes naturally.

the redemption of suffering

"I saw sorrow turning into clarity."

—YOKO ONO

In his book *No Future Without Forgiveness,* Desmond Tutu writes about Nelson Mandela as a man who was not broken but refined by his twenty-seven years of imprisonment in South Africa:

"Those twenty-seven years and all the suffering they entailed were the fires of the furnace that tempered his steel, that removed the dross. Perhaps without that suffering he would have been less able to be as compassionate and as magnanimous as he turned out to be. And that suffering on behalf of others gave him an authority and credibility that can be provided by nothing else in quite the same way."

We often feel burdened by what we have suffered or by our perception of others' cruelty toward us. We may sense that this suffering has broken us in irreparable ways. We may also feel plagued by our own transgressions, unkindness, failures, and regrets. We carry these burdens heavily in our hearts, perhaps feeling that the pain has cut so deeply the wound will never heal. This suffering comes to define us. We tell a story about who we are based on what we have suffered, much as recorded history is the story of suffering. This gives contours to our sense of self, and we replay the

43

images of what happened in our minds to keep this sense of self alive. "It's been awful, but at least it's *me*."

One moment of clear seeing frees us from imagination. There is a story of Alexander the Great who met the challenge of unraveling the Gordian knot by simply removing his sword and cutting through the thick cord. Just so, the blade of clarity cuts through without need for unraveling the knot. It is a moment of innocence—a moment of knowing that nothing in what we have experienced can ultimately define us, nothing can reduce us. The actual experience of who we are in this very moment is clear and unstained, despite the suffering we have endured or caused. We suddenly feel wide awake. Though memory is intact, there is a sense that the world seems fresh and new, and ourselves with it. We are baptized in our own shining awareness.

Frequently in Dharma Dialogues, people will speak of some form of abuse suffered either in childhood or thereafter. I often notice their eyes clouding over as they recount the story and the painful memory fills their awareness. The person becomes in his or her mind the one who was harmed and is now damaged. At this point, I usually ask the person to discover in the immediacy of the moment the awareness that is not suffering, despite the memory of the story. I then ask him or her to see if there was an awareness that was not involved in the suffering at the time of the event itself. In almost every case there is recognition of the witnessing presence that was not reacting to whatever was occurring, no matter how traumatic. In the moments of realizing that which was okay throughout every ordeal, the person's face lights up. Despite the painful memory, a haven of peace is always available.

For instance, many people who have lived through car accidents report that they experienced the accident as if in slow-motion awareness, just curiously watching themselves rolling about in the car or noticing odd things such as a bystander holding a red umbrella. It was not until later that fear and trauma were felt. Or, we might have received a call in the night telling us of a loved one's death. On the emotional level, a huge wave of grief forms and starts to well up inside. Yet on a subtler level of awareness, there was only the silent witnessing of hearing the words on the phone. This subtle awareness is accessible throughout every ordeal.

This is not to say that our suffering isn't real. At the time of its occurrence it is real enough. The point is to notice that it does not last, except in imagination. We relive the story of past suffering only in our minds. New and painful events may occur—and we do not deny the emotions connected with them—but these also pass in witnessing awareness. The Tibetans speak of the mythical bird known as the Garuda and how the path of its flight across the sky leaves no trace. Similarly, all the burdens of our heart are liberated in clear seeing and leave no trace. Nothing that arises in the sky defines or reduces the sky itself. In the same way, we are not ultimately defined or reduced by any experience.

If we allow our pain to be felt and freed, our suffering does great work in softening our hearts. It is, in the words of Trungpa Rinpoche, "manure for the field of wisdom." In fact, it is important to know that any difficult mind state is welcome to arise at any moment just as the sky welcomes whatever arises in it without resistance. Our suffering, if we feel it deeply and allow its natural passing, makes us stronger and yet more tender. We are whole not only despite what we have suffered but often because of it.

In awakened awareness we are also able to see others as whole, despite their burdens and difficulties. The Buddha said that the near enemy to compassion is pity. To pity others is to demean them in one's own mind. Feeling compassion for others in their struggles and problems is recognizing their undiminished radiant nature while at the same time offering sympathy and comfort. None of us like to be pitied, but most of us appreciate compassion and being seen as whole despite our problems.

In a dark and crowded Benares train station one night more than twenty years ago, I heard a beautiful song rising from a throng of people. Drawn to the sound, I discovered a disconcerting sight. A small boy with a short rope in one hand and a begging bowl in the other guided along the platform an old blind man who carried on his back a crippled leper. Slowly moving through the hot mob of people, they constituted what initially seemed to me a singular creature of misery, a multi-limbed calamity. But they were singing, each in his own harmony, such an enchanting melody that the sight of their burdens seemed at odds with the sound in the night. As I stood there, mesmerized by their song and by their enthusiasm, the vision all at once became beautiful. While they sang their hearts out, I saw each of them as perfectly whole and free.

healthy remorse

Tenderness sometimes comes through remorse. We can forgive ourselves more easily as we understand the ways we have acted in ignorance and then allow feelings of healthy remorse to flow through us. We might gently notice that we were doing the best we could, given our level of wisdom or lack of it at the time. This is not to justify or spiritually bypass any wrongdoing. It is simply to acknowledge that we could do no other than what we did at that time and then let the painful consequences of our unkind actions do their own work in deconditioning us from behaving in similar ways again.

This type of remorse should not be confused with guilt.

Healthy remorse is the unblinking recognition of words or actions that have caused pain and the resolve to be watchful of them should they arise again. Guilt usually has strong identification with it—"I am guilty"—as though we are reduced entirely to the harmful action, as though we are guiltiness itself. Believing that one is inherently guilty can produce an internal resignation that leads to even more confusion and harmful actions.

One of my lessons in remorse involved ingratitude born of fear. Traveling alone in Morocco in 1973, I found myself on an overnight bus journey coming down from the mountains to the plains. Not only was I the lone tourist and the only English-speaking person on the bus, but I was the only woman as well. Halfway through the journey a violent thunderstorm broke out, and the bus began to heave and lurch all over the dark and winding roads of the mountain pass. Driving rain made it impossible to see where the road ended and the steep cliffs began. We rode on like this in a tense silence for some time. Finally, in the middle of the night, the driver stopped near a small village. What was supposed to be a drop-off point for passengers now appeared to be the final destination for the night. Evidently the driver had decided that it was too dangerous to continue the journey. Everyone began to get off the bus and the driver indicated that I, too, must do likewise.

Now we were out in the thunderstorm itself and very quickly the men disappeared into the darkness heading toward the village; everyone, that is, except one man, who stayed behind and motioned for me to follow him. Using only rudimentary French, I made clear to him that I was interested in finding a *pension* in which to board for the night. But I had a sinking feeling that this place had nothing of the kind.

We made our way to the village, which consisted primarily of stone huts. I shouted the word *pension* at the back of my guide's head as we scuttled through the storm, and he never once acknowledged hearing me. After winding down many small alleys, the man opened the door to one of the huts, a one-room affair with no heat. In it a woman and several small children were asleep. The man spoke to them in Arabic and the woman and children moved with their blankets from the cot onto the floor. The man motioned for me to sit on the cot.

I stood in the doorway, irrationally furious that he had not led me to a *pension,* as though one should have magically appeared. Looking around at the dark empty street I knew that my options were few. Having heard many horrifying stories of what can happen to young women traveling alone in Morocco, I was terrified of entering the hut. But staying outside in the freezing rain for hours, with no sure safety there either, seemed worse. Frightened, cold, and desperate to get out of the storm, I ventured warily into the room and, removing only my outer coat, sat on the now vacant cot. I then pulled my Swiss Army Knife from my pack with a flourish and made sure that everyone saw it. After some murmuring the family went to sleep. I remained wide awake. Hours later at the first light of dawn, I rushed out into the rain and back to the bus, never giving a word of thanks.

A young frightened woman taken in by strangers, I was unable to recognize and show gratitude for the kindness that had been offered to me. Not only that, I had even been rude. Over the next days and weeks I reflected on my behavior of that night with strong feelings of remorse. I wished with all my heart that I had thanked those people.

Over the course of my life there have been hundreds of such lessons in remorse. Sometimes remorse comes from nothing more than speaking to someone and then noticing a small flicker of embarrassment or hurt in his or her eyes. These experiences of what I call healthy remorse serve to wear down our pride and make us willing to apologize or make amends as needed. They also allow us to understand the actions of those who behave in ways that are hurtful just as, when confronted by someone being ungrateful or rude, I now might recognize that frightened young woman in Morocco all those years ago who did the best she could at the time.

forgiveness

"If you want to see the brave, look at those who can forgive. If you want to see the heroic, look at those who can love in return for hatred."

— BHAGAVAD GITA

It is said that when a woman in a certain tribe in Africa becomes pregnant she goes to the wilderness with other women from her tribe to pray and meditate until they hear the song of the unborn child. They then return to the tribe and teach the song to the other members. When the baby is born, the tribe gathers around the newborn and sings the birth song. They sing it again when the child passes from adolescence into adulthood, at the time of marriage, and at the time of death. But there is one other time that a person's song is sung by his tribe. When a member of the tribe has caused suffering to another, he is put into the center of a circle around which his tribe gathers and sings his birth song to remind him of his own beauty. The tribe recognizes that love, not punishment, is the remedy for losing one's way.

How do we forget our beauty and engage in acts of suffering? In quiet observation of ourselves, we notice the ways conditioned or habitual thoughts based in past experience drive our impulses in the present. When these thoughts are based on suffering and confusion, the resulting actions usually make a mess of our lives. Transfixed by the thoughts, we stumble along making mistakes and enduring or causing all kinds of further suffering. The more intense the conditioned thoughts, the more confused are our actions in the present. In those moments, we have forgotten our true self.

For example, in a bad mood (conditioned negative thoughts usurping awareness), we say hurtful words to someone close to us. The person withdraws or angrily retorts, and we become enraged. We get into the car and recklessly speed down the highway, barely aware of driving, so lost now in the fervor of our story that we endanger the lives of everyone around us. The initial agitation of conditioned thoughts has now escalated into a fury, which will further produce its own conditioned thoughts.

In awakened awareness we attune to a silence that is beyond this conditioning. We also realize that conditioned thoughts come uninvited and sometimes overtake us. The more we recognize this in our own case, the more we start to realize that it is true of everyone. When people are behaving badly, it is because they have been overtaken by negative thoughts.

Just as our response to our children's idiosyncrasies and acts of confusion is one of magnanimity, we begin to feel generosity and understanding for our intimates, coworkers, and even strangers we hear about in the news—anyone lost in their mental conditioning. Knowing that no act defines us allows us to see that no action can ultimately define anyone else. We can look into the eyes of those with whom we have had difficulty and sense the pure presence that is beyond their words and actions. I recently saw some sidewalk graffiti that said: "The holiest spot on earth is one where an ancient hatred has become a present love."

However, forgiveness does not mean that we condone harmful actions. We may recognize that someone who has hurt us may do so again and we take all necessary precautions to avoid that recurrence. At the same time, we do so with the understanding that confusion, ignorance, and cruelty exist as manifestations of consciousness; indeed, we know well those flickers of madness in ourselves. Imagine if these little flickers had been hot coals of anger for as long as we could remember. We might feel impelled to act out our fury, feeling that we were about to explode. When I see someone enraged, I sometimes have the sense that the internal pressure—slowly boiling—has built up over time and is now erupting.

We can think of many despots in history who have instituted torture or committed genocide. We are now experiencing a worldwide rampage of terror propagated by people who want to inflict as much pain and suffering as they possibly can. We can know that the conditioned thought program in all of these cases was an unhappy one. Only a hellish state, a tormented mind, would cause such misery. Cruelty is only born of pain and confusion. It does not come from genuine happiness and love. As Longfellow observed, "If we could read the secret history of our enemies, we would find in each man's life a sorrow and a suffering enough to disarm all hostility."

We can understand how cruelty happens because we know the difficulty we sometimes experience in resisting impulses to say an unkind word or do an unkind deed. Despite our best efforts, we sometimes fail. How much harder is it for those whose conditioned thoughts are even more negative or whose circumstances have been unrelentingly difficult? When tenderness comes in such difficult cases, it is exceptionally beautiful.

About seven years ago, a man came to Dharma Dialogues having been just released from prison. An artist, aikido practitioner, and family man, he had grown a few marijuana plants in the field of his country residence. At dawn one morning thirty federal agents raided his home, terrifying his wife and two small children as they ripped apart every room. The man was taken to prison where he spent the next two and a half years. His house and property were confiscated. His wife, forced to repurchase their home, endured over the next years a tremendous financial struggle on half the usual income.

When the man was released from prison, he felt shame for having caused so much suffering to his family and bitterness at the justice system for imposing such a high price for his mistake. Six months after he began attending Dharma Dialogues, he showed up at one of our weeklong silent retreats on the Oregon coast.

"At that retreat," he later said, "forgiveness rolled out—both vast and specific. The silence and the group sessions were doing their work in tenderizing me, and one morning I started crying. It lasted for four hours. During that time my mind released itself into the suffering that I had experienced, the suffering that I had been tangential to, and the suffering that I had caused, especially the feelings that my children were having as a result of my actions. All the events from childhood to adulthood in which suffering occurred—all of it got rolled into forgiveness. The slate was cleaned. I felt deep humility as a human being who made mistakes. That understanding allowed me to feel forgiveness for everybody involved in my incarceration—the judges, the jailers, the probation officers. Yeah, I made mistakes and everybody makes mistakes, so what's to hold against anyone."

People say that it is hard to forgive, but holding onto bitterness is much harder. It is akin to being bitten by a snake. The initial bite—the grievance, let's say—is very painful, but the real problem comes with the venom coursing through one's system. The venom of hatred or resentment is usually much worse than the original bite; it seems to invade every cell of one's body. Forgiveness is the most powerful antidote for this condition. It is, as someone once said, "the fragrance left by the violet around the foot that just crushed it."

tender mercies

"So come my friends, be not afraid
We are so lightly here
It is in love that we are made
In love, we disappear."

—LEONARD COHEN, "BOOGIE STREET,"
FROM THE ALBUM *TEN NEW SONGS*

Soon after meeting Poonjaji in India, I witnessed an unforgettable event. During the morning session a woman who appeared to be in a state of hysteria came onto the platform with him. Her questions and comments seemed to have nothing to do with what he was teaching, but worse, she was flailing about, hysterically laughing, and practically knocking the master off his seat. Although he appeared as strong as a mountain, at that time Poonjaji was nearly eighty years old with various health ailments. It was almost too much for those of us sitting nearest him to bear, and at one point someone reached out to restrain the woman, fear-ing that the she might accidentally harm the master at any moment. Meanwhile, Poonjaji tried in poignant ways to get through to her. "You and I are the same," he said. "You need not be a beggar hoping to be saved; you are already on the throne of freedom." In response the woman squealed with laughter and threw her arms around his head, pulling him to her. After what seemed an eternity, she stood up to leave, but not before asking for his handkerchief, the only one he had with him with which to wipe his brow. Of course, he gave it to her, and with arms akimbo, laughing and bumping her way through the crowd while proudly waving the treasured handkerchief, the woman went back to her seat.

The people in the front rows collectively sighed in relief. "What a waste of his precious energy," I thought. "He should be protected from people like that. Those people need a therapist, not a Buddha."

As I was muttering to myself, a quiet transformation was occurring on the platform. Poonjaji had grown totally silent and closed his eyes, even though we were in the dialogue part of the morning's meeting. Those of us sitting near him then saw three or four tears roll down his cheeks.

It dawned on me that Poonjaji was not sitting in judgment, thinking about whether this person or that one was worthy of him or a drain of his life force. He was seeing only the suffering, the deep wounds which had turned into neurosis, the child who could not find her way home, even while standing in her own front yard. If he was comparing at all, he probably observed little difference between any of us. Taking on the blind forces of ignorance that lead to suffering, he was perhaps overcome by the immensity of it. Perhaps at that moment he could do nothing but shed a few tears. Ashamed of the harshness I had inwardly directed toward a woman whose mental capacity and trials in life were unknown to me, I felt my own judgment melting away. And I knew as I sat there that I would never again see anything as precious as Poonjaji's tears.

In releasing our judgments and assumptions about others, we find compassion in the most trying of circumstances. Compassion comes easily when we see a sick child or when someone we love is hurt or in trouble. But in awakened awareness, compassion flows for those who are seemingly the least likely recipients of it: "Jesus in his distressing disguises," as Mother Teresa put it.

A few years ago I was with a close woman friend in a grocery store in California. As we snaked along the aisles, we became aware of a mother with a small boy moving in the opposite direction and meeting us head on in each aisle. The woman barely noticed us because she was so furious at her little boy, who seemed intent on pulling items off the lower shelves. As the mother became more and more frustrated, she started to yell at the child and several aisles later had progressed to shaking him by the arm.

At this point my friend spoke up. A wonderful mother

of three and founder of a progressive school, she had probably never once in her life treated any child so harshly. I expected my friend would give this woman a solid mother-to-mother talk about controlling herself and about the effect this behavior has on a child. Braced for a confrontation, I felt a spike in my already elevated adrenaline.

Instead, my friend said, "What a beautiful little boy. How old is he?" The woman answered cautiously, "He's three." My friend went on to comment about how curious he seemed and how her own three children were just like him in the grocery store, pulling things off shelves, so interested in all the wonderful colors and packages. "He seems so bright and intelligent," my friend said. The woman had the boy in her arms by now and a shy smile came upon her face. Gently brushing his hair out of his eyes, she said, "Yes, he's very smart and curious, but sometimes he wears me out." My friend responded sympathetically, "Yes, they can do that; they are so full of energy."

As we walked away, I heard the mother speaking more kindly to the boy about getting home and cooking his dinner. "We'll have your favorite—macaroni and cheese," she told him.

Not needing to prove we are right or that someone else's behavior should be pointed out and punished, we often know instinctively what will be most conducive for harmony in a given situation, what will be most helpful to all concerned. To reprimand the mother may have incited her to even more anger—anger that may have been directed at the child later on. Although there are times when the appropriate action is to physically stop someone from hurting another, it is often helpful simply to show love and understanding as a reminder to those lost in anger.

There are possibilities for tender mercies for each one of us throughout our day. These small kindnesses to friends, family, or strangers may go unnoticed by the world. We may not win any awards for heroism or be written up in the newspaper for altruistic deeds, but we will exist in a self-generated field of sacredness by letting love flow through us. It is its own reward.

e m b o d i m e n t

Watercress. She saw it growing near the river's

edge, like tiny green lilies in woven clusters, float-

ing in the eddies. Her exhilaration of the previous

night and morning had sustained her so far, but

now she was hungry. She moved toward the plant,

an animal of pure instincts. As she tasted and

swallowed the watercress, she felt her body incorporate it into its own essence. Her corporeality, the flesh-and-blood-ness of herself, dominated her awareness as she chewed. She was a creature, dependent on the natural world for sustenance. She had been sculpted by nature to feel, and her survival depended on the fidelity of her senses and their messages from a continuous flux of pleasure and pain.

Her bodily sensations heightened, she felt as if she were being caressed by existence. The breeze on her face, the sun on her skin, the taste in her mouth; these were a cascade of sensations declaring her aliveness. She reflected on her sensuality, her reflections generated not by thinking but by receiving information from an awakened aspect of her own awareness.

She belonged here, on the ground, on the earth. Having once had the notion that embodiment was an obstacle to understanding, she had entertained beliefs of a transcendent reality that had no use for the manifest world. She had even attempted practices designed to release her from bodily concerns and to quash her natural desires.

Now it was so clear: embodiment is not in contradiction with divinity. It is divinity's explicit expression. Whatever sacredness, love, dignity, or pleasure she would ever know, she would experience through her body and this earth.

no transcendence

"May your view be as vast as the sky and your actions as fine as barley flour."

—PADMASAMBHAVA

To live in full embodiment of our humanness, in passionate presence, it is important to examine beliefs that might inhibit this full expression and to look at how we use them to avoid feeling deeply. One area of belief that can numb us is spiritual ideology.

Many spiritual traditions encourage disembodied transcendence or lofty detachment from the very things that make up a passionately engaged life. They place emphasis on the ephemeral nature of all phenomena, which is often misunderstood to mean that none of it matters much. Believing that this world is not real, adherents attempt to transcend any attachment to it and focus instead on the disembodied world of pure spirit as the only true reality. They yearn to escape what is seen as the illusory life of woe on earth to arrive at the promised land of eternal bliss—a spiritual upgrade to the life of the hereafter.

There is no rational reason to believe such promises and every reason to challenge them, based on the overwhelming evidence that the life we are living is the only life we know. When we think there is some other realm waiting for us, a better world somewhere else or some other time—heaven, the Absolute, or nirvana—we live in a sense of postponement, as though this is a dress rehearsal for our "eternal life." We fail to see that fundamentally we are embodied expressions of the animating force, not disembodied spirits trapped in flesh, awaiting final release.

Religious beliefs in transcendence have been handed down over time from superstitious societies, when most people led short, brutal lives and relied on hope for a better afterlife to get them through the day. But the disembodied worldview is not only anachronistic, it is potentially harmful. It can lead to apathy by dampening our passion for living and our care of others. Stifling our natural enjoyment of being human can result in depression—a sense of marking time in what is seen as the prison of illusion. Religious beliefs about a glorious afterlife can also induce susceptible people into committing atrocities on behalf of those who would manipulate them for that purpose.

In addition to the disembodied or transcendent worldview, there are spiritual schools that blithely declare, "It's all perfect." These traditions believe that everything that happens is God's will and exactly as it is supposed to be. Some of these schools say that all of manifestation is preordained, a future history already written, and that every flicker of your eyelid and every falling of a leaf is predetermined and therefore perfectly ordered to be. Whether or not manifestation is preordained, we may acknowledge that in the vast cosmic swirl in which galaxies come and go there is some sort of order, some governing laws of nature. From that vast sweep we see only perfection. Here on earth I prefer a Zen master's comment on the subject: "Even though it's all perfect, there's still room for improvement."

Yet another popular belief system is that of the law of karma. A variation on the "It's all perfect" theme, the belief in karma says that everything that happens to a person is due to prior causes in either this or a previous life. It says that we are each trailing an infinite wake of actions from previous births and that at any moment one of these actions may be the cause of, say, having a car accident, winning the lottery, or dialing a wrong number. Every moment of life is seen as the result of past karma.

These worldviews—it's all illusory, it's all perfect, it's all karma—can hide a cowardice of heart. They can be used to buffer our feelings for those who are suffering or who are less fortunate. Those who subscribe to the world-as-illusion belief often say of people who are suffering that it is not really happening; it is only a dream. Those who say that it's all perfect or preordained feel it is happening exactly as it is supposed to be, according to the will of God. And those who say it is due to karma might feel that misery is just, that those who are suffering somehow deserved it and are paying off a karmic debt.

These beliefs may also provide justification for people to take more than their share and to squander earth's dwindling resources. If it's not real, what does it matter if we lay waste to the planet? If it's all perfect, we are seemingly supposed to lay waste to the planet since that is what is happening. And if it is just karma, we enjoy our consumption guilt-free, feeling entitled according to our past good deeds.

While many people who subscribe to these belief systems may have a more sophisticated understanding of them and care deeply for others and for the earth, the belief systems themselves are often used as rationalizations for self-centered behavior by those with less mature understanding. We have all heard the platitudes of people upholding these world-views. Perhaps we have even bristled at times when we notice that those who shout them loudest are often in positions of privilege or have not been tested in the fires of loss.

In Dharma Dialogues one night a woman spoke about an event that had often caused her feelings of regret. She said that many years ago, when she was new to spiritual ideas, she lived next door to a pregnant woman with whom she hoped to develop a friendship. After the baby was due, the woman phoned the neighbor to initiate a visit. The neighbor was very appreciative of the call as she was grieving the loss of her baby. She sadly explained that the baby had been stillborn. The woman caller responded to this news with a short spiritual discourse about how everything is meant to be. Suddenly, the grieving mother became completely silent on the phone. They soon hung up and never spoke to each other again. Even though the caller was well intentioned in offering a spiritual perspective, her limited understanding caused separation.

The word "compassion" from its Latin roots means "to suffer with." True compassion actually feels the suffering of others. In awakened awareness there is no reassuring story that allows distancing from this suffering. The intelligence is clear and vast enough to contain it, yet specific and tender enough to be with the nuances of sorrow. It does not look away, nor does it rely on beliefs for an escape from feeling. After all, what kind of freedom demands an escape from suffering? Wouldn't real freedom include suffering?

At the same time, it is not necessary for the awareness to collapse into abject misery. Although our hearts may be merged with those who are suffering, we can offer them and ourselves the spacious awareness that knows that suffering is part of being alive. Rather than tightening in resistance, we simply feel whatever suffering presents itself and allow it to be released as it arises, moment by moment, without demanding that it should stop. It uncoils itself in the clear open space of awareness and goes of its own accord.

I once witnessed a true example of compassion in freedom. A sobbing woman came before Poonjaji and through her sobs told him that she had just heard tragic news. Her best friend had been working late in his office in Kathmandu, Nepal, the night before and some men had broken in and stabbed him repeatedly in the stomach. He was in critical condition in a Nepalese hospital, and the woman was leaving on the next train to go to him. She said that since hearing this news she felt she had daggers in her own stomach.

Taking her hands in his, Poonjaji looked at her in silence as she continued to cry, then putting his forehead to hers, he said simply, "I grieve with you." They sat together that way for quite some time and, as the woman's sobs subsided, Poonjaji then said, "But this is samsara." (*Samsara* in Sanskrit means "the cycle of life and death.")

The succinctness of that encounter has served as a reminder for me ever since. A willingness to deeply feel the suffering—I grieve with you—and also to acknowledge that this is how it is here; this is life in its horror and beauty. In understanding our situation from a vast perspective, yet feeling it in its specific and personal displays, our motivation becomes that of service informed by awakened awareness—our view as vast as the sky, our actions as fine as barley flour.

deep ecology, wide self

"If you wish to make an apple pie from scratch, you must first create the universe."

—CARL SAGAN

Although many of us in the wealthier parts of the world are currently enjoying longer life spans and access to information, comfort, and unprecedented wealth, there are also ominous signs everywhere we turn. We are faced with challenges previously unknown in history: global warming, dying oceans, species extinctions, ozone depletion, lack of fresh water, a worldwide human population explosion resulting in competition for scarce resources, and potential for violence due to those pressures. What makes our time unique is the global nature of the problems. There is nowhere left to run.

There are now large ecological movements professing philosophies of conservation, promoting policies of sustainability or even no economic growth, and challenging the homogenization and tyranny of global economics. But without a change in our hearts and a true awakening of empathy, all the best ideas in the world will make little difference. Pointing out the problems to those who seem unaware of them or asking for sacrifice on the part of those who are informed does not inspire change.

Despite our lofty strategies and philosophies, humans are still largely driven by primitive instincts of aggression and greed. Our ancient biological program triggers overly protective fight-or-flight responses to the most insignificant of situations, as though being cut off on the freeway is equivalent to being chased by a mastodon. And though it seems like a good idea to live more simply and to share equitably, our survival programming prefers that we take more for ourselves. While these impulses have historically allowed the human race to multiply when resources were abundant and the population was scant, the drive for self-preservation and self-gratification at all costs is becoming contraindicated for the health of planetary life in general.

Just as we are careful about not using spiritual ideology to distance us from the suffering of our world, we must also address the limitations of environmental or eco-philosophy when it is devoid of a spiritual perspective. Spiritual philosophies tend to float our awareness into clouds of denial. Environmental philosophies sometimes mire us in a fixation on a purely biological reality. We may neglect the larger view, the dimensions of understanding and love, while being overly attached to our own environmental goals. Failing to consider the web of complication in effecting those goals, or the feelings of those who will be affected by them in present reality, often causes adversarial responses in communities, preventing the very outcomes we hope to achieve.

Our first step in effecting change is to find love in our hearts and to offer that love in all negotiations. We must also model our values by the example of our lives. As Gandhi said, let us be the change we want to see. A friend once commented, "Any fool can see that we are in a global ecological crisis. The question is, how do we make a fool care." We make a fool care by encouraging the wise one living within the fool to come forth. The wise one already cares. All that is required is that we honor and live by that shining wisdom which, despite our foolishness, passionately exists within us.

Most of us know when we are behaving selfishly. It doesn't feel good and we may have twinges of regret, but the force of conditioning often compels us to persist in the behavior, to take more than our share, to ignore the costs to others or to our environment. Likewise, we know when we are living in hypocrisy, proclaiming values that we ourselves do not embody. Feeling the discomfort of these situations is awakened awareness itself. If we gently allow these feelings into full consciousness, our own heart intelligence overcomes the tendency to compromise our integrity and demands of us an alignment between what we say and how we live.

A woman once came to Gandhi and asked him to please tell her son to give up eating sugar. Gandhi asked the woman to bring the boy back in a week. Exactly one week later the woman returned, and Gandhi said to the boy,

"Please give up eating sugar." The woman thanked the Mahatma and, as she turned to go, asked him why he had not said those words a week ago. Gandhi replied, "Because a week ago, *I* had not given up eating sugar."

Many of us have an understanding of the high costs to the ecosystem that our lives represent, especially in the richer countries where we consume the largest share of the planet's resources. Yet without deeply caring about those who are affected by our disproportionate consumption, it is difficult to give up our rich way of life, and this makes it untenable for us to preach to others about cutting back.

When people first arrive at our retreats, they are asked to sign up for a small volunteer job. It might be to help wash the dishes or ring a bell for meetings—any one of the many simple tasks required to run a large retreat. On the first day many volunteer slots are often left unfilled. But as the days pass, not only are all the volunteer spaces filled, help begins to flow in every possible way. One person fixes a creaky door; another helps an elderly person walk to all the events; several people take turns feeding a woman with a broken arm; another gathers fallen wood from the forest to spare the retreat facility's wood supply; and a thousand other kindnesses occur anonymously and go unnoticed. Even though we are in silence, there is a palpable feeling of interconnectedness that is rarely matched in conversations *about* interconnectedness. This feeling naturally inspires happiness, and generosity flows out of joy.

What is the perspective that allows us to embody true ecological consciousness, to live lightly on this earth, to align our actions with our values, to consider the greater good? In quiet witnessing presence, we can actually feel our own embodiment inextricably connected to the atmosphere: our breath going in and out, exchanging atoms; the sunlight in the food we eat to sustain us; the myriad systems of rain and evaporation mingling in our own hydration. We look into the eyes of another creature, human or not, and we see there the timeless quality of being. We notice the plant pushing up out of the sidewalk and immediately feel the same force of life that we ourselves embody. Even the cement through which the plant pushed reflects a dance of molecules, just as we reflect a dance of molecules moving in and out of our bodies. The people who are starving in poisoned deserts, the dying seabirds covered in oil from a spill, and the loggers cutting the last of the old growth trees out of fear for their own economic survival are not just some other creatures; they are *us*.

As we tune into the deeper life rhythms, we no longer depend on philosophy to tell us that we are interdependent. We viscerally experience ourselves as inseparable from our surroundings. In this recognition, whatever is in our awareness takes on a hue of familiarity—of family. Our sense of self widens. Our selfishness may continue as a genetic predisposition, but what we define as self may become as wide as the universe. Just as we happily and without thinking want to share with our children or extended family, we feel concern for and generosity toward the family of beings. Our actions are born of wanting the greatest good for all, and we address any differences we have with the tenderness and respect one accords to close relatives. The boundaries between who is family and who is not begin to blur, and suddenly one feels intimate with existence itself. In this feeling of belonging, we realize that we don't need as much for happiness as we once thought and that it is far more enjoyable to share than to hoard.

Poonjaji, for example, exemplified an innate sensitivity to the environment without, to my knowledge, any study of environmental philosophy. He lived in a small rented house with several other people. He often wrote a letter of reply on the back of the original letter sent to him and would usually reuse the envelope as well. All garbage from the house would be thrown to the pigs on the street, and there was almost no other waste that required dump disposal. Until his legs gave out in the last few years of his life, he walked nearly everywhere he went. Once, a friend and I gave him a large basket of beautiful and colorful gifts for his house—toiletries, towels, sheets, kitchen items. Even as we left them on the doorstep, I knew they seemed out of place in the simple austerity of his home. By the following day, he had given away every single thing.

Poonjaji often said, "All is your own Self." This realization—Self unto Self—is our best hope for survival. Knowing this, we care for our world and its inhabitants, not out of ideology but out of love.

awakened sensuality

"Feels like lightning running through my veins . . ."
—DAVID GRAY, "PLEASE FORGIVE ME,"
FROM THE ALBUM *WHITE LADDER*

In wakefulness we exist in a divine affair of the senses. Smell, taste, touch, sound, and feelings are all heightened because our awareness is not drained by obsessive thinking and is therefore free to experience the full range of bodily and emotional sensations. Though thoughts continue to arise, they do not transfix us, and our attention is available for the rich array of sensations that life offers. Our sensual appreciation intensifies in wakefulness and becomes more and more refined.

This type of sensuality differs from a gluttonous or hungry attachment to the world of sense pleasures, as is sometimes associated with notions of sensuality. What is often pursued in the name of sense pleasure is an attempt to drown out the din of a troubled mind as people try, sometimes in reckless and desperate ways, to divert attention from their mental projections and depressing stories.

On a train from the countryside into London one day I sat opposite a young man wearing stereo earphones. The noise coming from his headset, intended for his ears only, was loud enough for everyone in the train car to hear, a screeching sound like a dental drill directly next to one's ear. I wondered if the young man was partly deaf. When he spoke on his cell phone, I realized that he wasn't deaf, but I suspected that he soon would be. Next I wondered what the poor fellow was attempting to drown out in his mind by using such an extreme decibel level of sound.

When we are very loud inside, we require external amplification to distract us from the internal roar, and we often pursue this amplification through the senses. As both the internal and external roars increase, we become even more desensitized and require a still greater barrage of sensations to forget ourselves. We can see the effects of desensitization in our culture's indulgence in violent movies, violent music, shock TV, dangerous sex, and addictions to speed and intoxicants. We see our young women replace their true sensuality with fame obsession, dieting, drugs, and superficial sex. We see our young men craving violence in video games, sports, and media. All of this signifies a deadening of sensitivity, a disassociation from life itself.

Awakened awareness, on the other hand, celebrates the

subtleties of the senses and makes more delicate our appreciation of all things. When we are at ease and quiet, our capacity for sense pleasure increases while the amount of stimulation required for the pleasure concomitantly decreases. In other words, a little goes a long way.

This is particularly noticeable in silent retreats. As people relax in simple presence—just *being* without the need to be this or that—they wake up, as though from the dead, into a lush world of sensations. People often describe food as never having tasted so good. They might notice how a heightened sense of smell evokes feelings and memories from childhood, or how colors appear remarkably vivid. Could a leaf have ever been so *green*?

The simplest pleasures fill our hearts with great joy. I once sat in silence on a porch with a group of students during a retreat as we watched two middle-aged women on the front lawn, fellow retreatants, taking turns pushing each other on a swing for the best part of an hour. Leaning back with toes to the sky and the sun on their faces, they went higher and higher, quietly giggling now and again. Unbeknownst to the women, the porch observers all shared in their delight, conspiratorially smiling and winking at each other.

We don't need to be in silent retreat to experience heightened sensations. We can allow our awareness to rest in ease and quietude no matter what is going on around us. Awareness will then be naturally awake and responsive to the surroundings. At any moment we can directly experience being touched by the world—air touching our skin, light touching our eyes, sound touching our ears. In the middle of a crowd, a friend or lover takes our hand and thousands of signals run through our nervous system. In wakeful presence, we experience the intensity of those signals "like lightning running through my veins." If we are lost in thought, we barely notice. Awakened awareness also suffuses our sexuality with a sense of totality, a free sample of a mystical experience—"the workingman's taste of God" as writer Georg Feuerstein once put it.

The word "sentience" comes from Latin and means "to feel." We inhabit our bodies, relying on instincts, moving in the world as "enlightened" animals with all the sense doors flung wide open yet also with an understanding of our place in it. We then experience a thrilling sense of connection such that we might have the thought, "This is life at last."

As our senses become more acute, our responses to other beings become more refined. At one of our retreats some years ago, a man named Mick described an experience he had once had of awakened sensuality shared with a hummingbird. Working in his studio in the woods, he noticed that a hummingbird had flown in through the open door and had become trapped inside, searching for a way out and bumping into the overhead skylight. Mick opened the windows to his studio, but the bird could not manage to find them. After some time, the bird seemed quite distressed.

Mick was standing very still watching the bird, not wanting to frighten it any further, when suddenly, the hummingbird flew right up to within inches of his face and hovered
there for a few seconds—the two creatures, man and bird,
just looking at each other. Slowly, Mick raised his forefinger
and the bird alighted on it, a delicate breath of sensation. He
then carefully walked some thirty feet across the room and
out the door, in relaxed harmony with the little being on his
finger. Once outside, the hummingbird stroked his finger
several times with its bill before lifting off.

quiet dignity

In whatever situation we find ourselves, dignity is the one
treasure that cannot be taken from us. With it, we may be
stripped of everything, yet feel like a mountain. Without it,
we may have everything, yet feel like a pebble. We can
imagine the dignity of the Roman philosopher Boethius
during his incarceration as a political prisoner in A.D. 524.
During the last year of his life, while awaiting torture and
execution for charges of treason, he wrote one of the great
philosophical works of history, *The Consolation of Philosophy*. In it he said, "The only way one man can exercise
power over another is over his body and what is inferior to

it, his possessions. You cannot impose anything on a free mind, and you cannot move from its state of inner tranquility a mind at peace with itself."

We might also picture Gandhi, some fourteen hundred years later, wearing a simple loincloth and sitting in his stark Indian jail cell, the embodiment of true nobility. His was not the dignity that is sometimes mistaken for pride but the willingness to embody both fairness and kindness without compromise. In his example we also see that the willingness to see dignity in others can, in some cases, inspire more dignified behavior on their part. After a three-month stay in England to discuss India's independence (which would not come for sixteen more years), Gandhi said, "I have been convinced more than ever that human nature is much the same, no matter under what clime it flourishes, and that if you approached people with trust and affection you would have tenfold trust and thousandfold affection returned to you."

Dignity comes from self-respect and the habit of according respect to others. More often than not it remains anonymous, as it has no need to call attention to itself. A few years ago I formed a friendship with Tom, the father of one of our Irish friends of Dharma Dialogues. Because he is generally a quiet man, it was some time before I began to appreciate his wonderful insights on just about every subject we chanced upon. I also noticed how carefully he listened to whoever was speaking, be it a child or an adult. Now in his mid-nineties, Tom lives where he has for his entire life, a mile or two from the River Shannon in rural Ireland. He has rarely left this area, but he has a life rich in everything good that life offers—family, community, and a close relationship to the land that he has farmed for seven decades. Vital and alive, with an Irish twinkle in his eyes, he still goes dancing on Saturday nights in the village hall and sometimes doesn't return until after midnight.

Whenever Tom is in the room, I sense something that I associate with old world values, when people were not judged by the amount of their possessions but by the goodness and dignity of their lives in community. Tom's example reminds me of a poem by the Chinese philosopher Chuang Tzu called "When Life Was Full, There Was No History." It seems likely that most of the truly great ones who have lived on this earth have made no history. Their gentle lives were not recorded.

Dignity also manifests in circumstances that on the surface might be seen as humiliating. We sometimes see unusual dignity embodied, for instance, in a very old or sick person who, having lost all independence of movement, relies on others' help in the same way as an infant, yet exhibits a strength of character that transcends the infirmity of the body.

We even see dignity in circumstances that might, on the surface, seem truly pitiful. Many years ago two friends and I spent an afternoon visiting a leper community in

India dedicated to the production of crafts. What struck me most was how normal the community felt; people just going about their business, working on different projects in various areas of the compound, conversation and laughter sprinkled throughout. I became intrigued by a young woman of perhaps twenty—movie star beautiful—who, though she was missing all her fingers, radiated joyful presence. At the end of the day, we asked the community if we might take their picture. The group rallied with great enthusiasm, bustling about and changing out of work clothes into fineries. I kept an eye on the beautiful girl as she negotiated a brush through her long dark hair, using the two palms of her hands. When it came time for the photograph, she carefully placed her hands behind her back and beamed a smile that lit up the sky.

sacred ground

*"This earth where we stand is the pure lotus land
And this very body, the body of Buddha."*
— "ZAZEN WASAN (SONG OF ZAZEN)" BY HAKUIN

People often speak about holy or sacred places. Some are mountains, such as Mount Kailash in Tibet, or Arunachala in southern India. Some are the sites of shrines or temples, some are deserts. But what really makes a place sacred? Is it that people from another time declared it so and followers have been worshipping there for centuries, or that the sunlight plays on a particular hillside in an unusual way, or that someone was once healed there? Or is it our own pure presence and our willingness to see that presence shining in everything that makes any spot of ground holy?

In 1977, I went to Calcutta to visit Dipa-ma, my first woman teacher. I was studying Buddhism at that time and had heard many stories of Dipa-ma and of the difficulties she had known and overcome in life. Many years before, she had lost two of her three children as well as her beloved husband in a short span of time. She developed a serious cardiac condition and, concerned that she would die "of a broken heart," her doctor suggested that she learn to meditate in one of Burma's many Buddhist centers. In grief she went off to the monastery and, after a period of meditation practice, emerged in clarity. Her losses had alchemized into compassion and she understood that her awareness could rest in pure presence, the only true sanctuary. She returned to her original home of Calcutta where she lived until the time of her death, spending time with her daughter and grandchild and seeing the occasional student who passed through.

Dipa-ma's second-floor apartment was on a narrow alley prone to flooding. To get there, one sometimes had to walk in nearly ankle-deep water through the alley, all the while mindful of the large rats for which Calcutta is famous. The building itself, made of unfinished concrete, in its run-down decrepitude had only the semblance of being old, without the charm. As one walked up the stairs, smells of all kinds assaulted one's senses, and the noise from the apartment complex and street below gave the atmosphere a carnival-like feeling of chaos.

Dipa-ma's flat consisted of one room, painted white, the size of a large bathroom in the west. It contained a desk, a few chairs, a bed, and a small cooking table. Dipa-ma always wore a plain white sari and looked older than her years. She was a very quiet woman whose loving presence left little to say. We often fell into silence together there in her simple abode. During these times the din of noise surrounding us outside seemed the most pleasant of sounds and a feeling of well-being would overcome me. At some point she would offer tea and sweets, and we would discuss dharma points.

It is now twenty-five years since I sat with Dipa-ma in Calcutta. My memory of our conversations has long since faded. But what has grown stronger in memory with the passage of time is a quality of light in being with her, though this is not a visual experience. It is the luminosity of *being*. Her embodiment of pure presence and the compassion that exuded from her created a feeling of sacredness unmatched by any cathedral, in my experience. Leaving

Dipa-ma in those days, I would walk back to my hotel through the alleys of Calcutta, every step on holy ground.

generosity

I went to Burma for the first time in the mid-1970s when one could obtain a visa for seven days only. Burma at that time was a mysterious and isolated country, as it remains to this day. However, unlike today, it was very peaceful back then, a fairy-tale land of ancient white temples in a lush green countryside. The city of Rangoon at that time was a mixture of antiquity and contemporary dilapidation. Golden pagodas thousands of years old shone amid unhurried streets of small shop stalls, oxen carts, and vehicles from the fifties. The only decent hotel for Westerners at that time was The Strand, a rundown colonial-style building which dated from the time of the British empire.

Our group of twelve friends had gone to Rangoon to meet Mahasi Sayadaw, head of the *sattipathana vipassana* (insight) tradition of Buddhism, in which we were studying. However, we discovered upon our arrival there that Mahasi had gone to his forest monastery in the upper wilds of Burma. Determined to meet him, our group flew the next day to Mandalay and hired a truck to take us the rest of the way to the remote village where we heard he would be. The journey took about twenty hours each way, precious time out of the one-week visa.

Mahasi Sayadaw's country monastery was a place practically untouched by the twentieth century. During our two days there we stayed in thatched huts of utmost simplicity, mosquito nets being the only concession to modern convenience. We had several sessions of teachings with Mahasi Sayadaw and otherwise enjoyed the quietude of the retreat center. However, I was most delighted by the young girls who swarmed around us in the women's quarters of the monastery. They had never before seen Westerners and were fascinated by our white skin as well as by the blond hair of some members of our group. Everywhere we went on the grounds of the compound, little hands stole touches of our skin and hair.

Though I had come this long distance for the teachings of a famous meditation master, the real teaching of that trip was to come from an unexpected source, for it was with the young girls that I experienced a lesson that I have never forgotten. As we were piling into the truck at the time of our departure, some of the girls who had been caring for us in the women's quarters came running with a little packet for each of the women in our group. The packets contained several cotton balls soaked in expensive Western perfume.

At that time perfume was difficult and expensive to come by even in Rangoon, a place that none of these girls had ever visited. I could only imagine how rare it was here in this small faraway village. Perfume may as well have been a substance from outer space. The Burmese girls had offered us what was most likely their greatest possession.

Our truck pulled away and they stood smiling as we waved at them while sniffing our perfumed cotton balls. And in their shining eyes, I glimpsed some kind of holiness. Never in my life had a gift had such value. For the intrinsic worth of any gift is not in the gift itself but in the heart of the giver.

The Buddha spoke about three kinds of giving: beggarly giving, friendly giving, and kingly giving. Beggarly giving is when we give the least of what we have. We give what we don't really need, what we would never miss, what we might have otherwise thrown away. Friendly giving is when we give what we use and like—not our very best— but that which we can afford and might appreciate having as a gift ourselves. Kingly giving is of a different order altogether. It is when we give the very best of what we have, when we give more than we keep for ourselves, when we give more than it seems we can afford, when we give with no expectation of reciprocity. In awakened awareness we give because the joy of generosity far exceeds the paltry satisfaction of hoarding or displaying wealth. We give because this very life is a gift itself and wants to be completely used up, wants to spread its perfume around everyone it meets.

awakened relationship

*"Oneness and otherness. It is impossible to speak or to think
without embracing both."*

— RALPH WALDO EMERSON

A powerful myth in our culture tells us that happiness lies
in romantic love. We grow up listening to songs on the
radio, watching movies, and reading novels that are about
finding love, keeping love, losing love. We dream that there
is that one out there—our soul mate—who will fulfill us
and bring us lasting happiness.

For many years the domain of romantic love constantly
occupied my mind. Beginning at the age of ten I fixated on
thoughts of romance and sex in a secret fantasy realm
which I now recognize as a longing for belonging. I tried to
fulfill this yearning in mostly tragic relationships that felt
suspiciously similar to the pain of my childhood. I would be
inexorably drawn to those who would reenact the kinds of
emotional abuse I had suffered as a child. Perhaps this was
an attempt to redeem all that sorrow, to play it over again,
to finally get it right. Or perhaps it was the force that compels us toward the familiar in relationships, no matter how
unhealthy. Though many of these relationships were in-
tensely passionate, I eventually learned that "animal mag-
netism" wasn't all that it was cracked up to be.

While hoping to assuage the pain of childhood can propel us into relationship, we also sometimes seek relationship because we don't feel whole in ourselves. We sense an emptiness inside and we want desperately to fill it. Something is missing; it must be our other half. Consequently, many relationships are based on the idea of two halves forming a whole. People become so dependent on each other that it is very common for a grieving spouse to die within six months of the passing of his "other half." One could say there is a beauty in that kind of bonding. I have been deeply touched over the years by many stories of grieving spouses "dying of a broken heart," not only among humans but also among whales, dogs, and other creatures. While we can appreciate that kind of bonding, we can also see its limitations. It is akin to two trees collapsed onto each other in a forest, each holding the other up, neither of them standing on their own. When one falls, both go down. Mikhail Naimy, friend and biographer of Kahlil Gibran, wrote, "The love that singles out a fraction of the whole foredooms itself to grief."

This kind of dependency can also foment smallness of mind and heart. Jealousy, resentment, and manipulation thrive in dependent relationships. It is as a business contract that says, "I'll love you if there's something in it for me," or "I'll love you if we can put our lives together in a way that works for me." More insidious for many couples is the day-to-day tedium of living with their spouses as polite strangers, a condition made possible only by fear of loneliness and not realizing how very lonely such a way of life actually is. These people live as shadows of themselves, acquiescing to the lowest common denominator of détente with their partner, neither of them able to creatively express themselves or feel any passion about life.

Relationship informed by awakened awareness is altogether different because it is not born of pain, dependency, or fear of loneliness; it is born of celebration. In awakened awareness it is understood that we are each, though unique expressions of one source, totally alone. It is the paradox of existence: no two alike, yet no two at all. What we may have formerly sensed as emptiness begging to be filled, we now experience as openness welcoming whatever comes but otherwise enjoying a vast sense of space. Coming to terms with that understanding means living in the full autonomy of wholeness. Our relationships are then imbued primarily with appreciation. We sense ourselves flowing along with a particular partner or friend, and we feel like two streams merging in and out of each other. Sometimes the streams intermingle; sometimes they part and stream in different directions. Neither stream needs the other's existence to be a stream in itself, yet when the two streams come together, there is a happy surge of bubbles that may last a moment or a lifetime.

Sexuality in a true and trusting partnership is a way of accessing the primeval, a place where wildness can emerge

and give expression to itself. It is also a safe haven for our
most tender and delicate of moments. In awakened sexuality, partners are at play with the archetypal forces of the
universe—the masculine and feminine principles. Just as
the yin/yang symbol has a tiny bit of yin in the yang and a
small bit of yang in the yin, partners may dance as and occasionally switch the classic roles of male and female. It is a
way of understanding "otherness," an understanding that
transcends the bedroom by giving us a peek into maleness
or femaleness that informs daily life. We often observe how
two people who have lived together a long time may be
softened or strengthened by each other in wonderful ways.
In awakened partnership, this influence is welcomed and is
not a cause for battle within the relationship. As a female
she incorporates some of his masculinity in herself; as a
male he takes in and is influenced by her femininity. The
yin/yang principles may operate in homosexual love as well.
Yet even as intimacy reaches its heights between two people, there is always the mystery of *other*.

Ultimately, however, we must recognize that whatever
we call *other* exists as part of the whole. In wholeness, we are
able to consider what is best for those we love without worrying over the question, How is this going to affect *me*? Because we enjoy what comes and are able to let go what goes,
our need for anything to go a particular way diminishes
greatly. We delight in another's delight and champion that
person's right to follow his or her own journey wherever it

may lead, with or without *me*. Just as a loving parent, with tears in her eyes, sees her son off to college when he leaves the nest, she also celebrates his solo flight, and her heart soars with dreams and possibilities for him. In the same way, we can soar in our relationships, however they play out, when we love in freedom.

organic death

"Earth to earth, ashes to ashes, dust to dust . . ."
—THE BOOK OF COMMON PRAYER

I first went to India in 1976, traveling overland from Europe with two friends, a journey of several months that required stays in places such as Turkey, Iran, Afghanistan, and Pakistan. It was an arduous trip. By the time we arrived in India, we were ready for the relative gentleness of the predominantly Hindu culture and excited to learn more of its customs.

We headed to Benares, the Hindu holy city, famous for its burning ghats. For five thousand years, Hindus have considered Benares to be the most auspicious place to have one's body cremated and one's ashes thrown into the

Ganges River. On our first night there, we made our way down to the main ghat on the Ganges, all the while hearing the hauntingly melodious chants sung by Indian pallbearers as they brought bodies to the funeral pyres.

There were eight bodies burning at the main ghat when we arrived. Several more were lying on planks nearby, some of them wrapped in beautiful saris, some of them in plain cotton cloth. All onlookers were silent, and only the chanting, the crackling fires, and the rushing river could be heard. As I took in the scene before my eyes, I knew that something inside of me was irreversibly shifting to accommodate the vision. But my reverie was broken when an Indian man in a shabby suit tapped me on the arm and asked, "Have you come here to watch the bodies burn?"

As this was precisely what I was doing at the moment he interrupted, the question seemed inane, and I resented the intrusion. I had also begun to lose patience with the various ploys for conversation that I had experienced as a Western woman after several months on the road overland to India. "Yes," I snapped back, to which the man nodded politely and said no more.

As I turned back to the funeral pyres, the sting of my rudeness began to pierce me. Here in the very presence of death, petty irritations seemed particularly absurd. I turned back to the man in the shabby suit in a gesture of reconciliation. Unable to think of anything more appropriate to say, I put the same question to him: "Have *you* come here to watch the bodies burn?"

"Well, that one in the middle there is my mother," he said in a friendly, matter-of-fact tone. "She died this morning in our village and her last words, whispered in my ear, were, 'Take my body to Benares.' I borrowed a car from my cousin and have been driving all day to bring her here."

I was taken aback at this news and managed a few more words of conversation, mindful that our chat should not go on too long under the circumstances but also wanting to offer the man the comfort of a little company, if only from a stranger. After a short time, we both turned back to the fire, and now my attention was drawn to the body in the middle, the man's mother. The grand reflections I had been having about death, the impermanence of all phenomena, and the preciousness of life transmuted into a more personal scale. The woman whose body was burning in front of me had been a wife, a mother, a daughter. Her dreams and stories could have perhaps filled a library, however simple her life might have seemed. But in the end the earth and wind would claim her—ashes to ashes, dust to dust. And before too long, no one would remember her name.

Leaving the ghats that night I had, for the first time in my life, an organic sense of death. I appreciated nature's necessity for life to flow through birth, being, and death to make room for more life to flow through the cycle of existence as well. Birth and death are but momentary punctuations of this cycle, two ends of a spectrum of being that takes place within a greater whole. And yet, how utterly unique the expression of each life—a cosmic story whispered only once. All that is left for us is to fully live it.

genuineness

The sun was directly overhead. She spied a river pool upstream, a place where the water was calm. Thirsty again, she went there to drink and to cool her face. As she bent with cupped hands, she noticed the clarity of the water. She could see ferns growing from the riverbed below and small fish

97

swimming around them. The water magnified their shapes and colors into magical enhancements of themselves. Superimposed on the surface, she saw the reflection of her face.

It had been a long time since she had truly seen her own face. She had seen mirrors and reflecting surfaces countless times, but she always had a story that went with the sight of her face. Emerging entirely from imagination, the story had little to do with present reality. Nevertheless, her attention had been mostly on the drama of it, her face serving as a floating image in the mirror before her, giving the story dimension and reflecting its various aspects—sadness, regret, longing.

She now understood how her internal story had created a mask, a visage she had presented to the world as though she were the central character in a play. The world, for its part, had provided her with continual situations in which to practice her role. But the character was lonely to maintain and challenging to love.

Now there she was, after a long journey, seeing in the water a face that reminded her of a time before the quest, a face similar to that of a child. It had no mask, no entrancing story. There was no faraway, driven, or haunted look in the eyes of this face. She realized that it would be fine to live with virtually no narrative and no idea of a central character. Strangely, she felt more than ever herself. She smiled at the reflection in the water.

burned into gold

"What is to give light must endure burning."

—VIKTOR FRANKL

When we are genuine, our successes are seen as gifts from existence and leave us feeling humbled. We know that we cannot claim credit for gifts with which we were endowed, no matter how much others would like to credit us for them. One may be a great singer, another a great surfer, and another a great shoe repairman. Seen from outside it may appear that we have chosen and cultivated our talents, but we each know inside ourselves that we seem gifted simply because we are the *beneficiaries* of a gift. A gift that comes from an unknown source. Knowing our talents are simply gifts we have received brings with it authenticity and humility in our expressions. It also allows us to appreciate the talents seen in those around us as expressions of the same universal source, and we can only marvel at its endless creativity. We see the manifold expressions of talent streaming through everyone, and we share in the delight of these expressions. Through the receipt of our own talents and through the delightful experience of appreciating the talents and gifts of others, we are continually reminded of our genuine nature, through which flows the universal creative force. The greater the creativity, the more we can sense the quiet authenticity of simply being, the calm within a river of artistry. We sometimes see in talented people a deep and quiet humility. Their awareness is at ease in true nature and lives in gratitude for the gifts they enjoy. These are lovely and fortunate doorways to authenticity.

But the fires of suffering and loss are particularly effective in bringing out what is most genuine in us. When our strategies are not working and our losses are piling up, we may be forced into our innermost depths where there is only the silence of being, our most genuine true nature. In awakened awareness, this innermost depth becomes the final refuge. It is akin to the smelting process of refining gold ore. All impurities are burned from the ore until there is only pure gold. In a similar way, awakened awareness lets suffering burn up everything that is holding on, everything that is not genuine and true, until all that is left is our pure shining essence.

Years ago I went through the painful ending and loss of a relationship which triggered a cascade of other losses in my life such that I ended up homeless, jobless, and almost penniless. Moreover, this phase of loss induced memories of seemingly every other great sorrow I had suffered since early childhood. Each thought of the past was tinged with regret accompanied by visions of missed opportunities, a sense of time wasted and misspent, and a feeling that I had been unlucky in life. Even thoughts of happy times past brought only sadness at how fleeting they had been and how little I had appreciated them at the time. On the other hand, thoughts of the future produced fear and a heaviness of heart, as though I were soldiering on in a war. It became clear that no mental toe step into thoughts of past or future would be safe. In each case there were scary stories about what had happened to me in the past or what I might become in the future.

Due to its extreme unpleasantness and not to any heroic efforts on my part, the habit of thinking about myself in the past and future slowly began to drop away. I could find relief only in present awareness where everything was basically just fine. The suffering with these mental pictures burned itself out simply through the process of suffering itself. It became as a hot fiery coal that could no longer be held in one's hand. The awareness had done all the work. It had seen through the fear, lament, and regret because it had fallen in love with the ease of its true self, its genuine nature, and it could no longer entertain madness.

In Dharma Dialogues I liken this to swimming in a clear glacier lake. A perfect temperature, the lake is clean and blue with visibility to its deep bottom and a smell of fresh aerated water. The trees around the lake swish and sway and perfume the air with green cool freshness. Now suppose you have grown up swimming in the neighborhood mud hole and know nothing about the glacier lake. The mud hole is polluted and dark, full of creepy crawlers and debris, and gives off an unpleasant odor. However, most of the neighborhood swims there and you have grown accustomed to it.

One day someone shows you the glacier lake. You are astounded that such beauty exists and that it was there all this time. You swim in it for hours and emerge exhilarated.

Now, when you next go to the mud hole it seems particularly awful. It hasn't changed, but you have. You have found a greater love—the glacier lake. The mud hole seems worse only in comparison to the beautiful lake. And the lake begins to haunt you. You can't get it out of your mind, and you can no longer tolerate the mud hole. The more time you spend at the glacier lake, the less possible it is to be at the mud hole. Like this, when we are used to living in our genuine self, the glacier lake of being, it becomes impossible to spend much time in the mud hole of morbid mind habits.

I have always appreciated the way older people seem, on the whole, to be more relaxed in themselves, more comfortable with who they are. They usually cannot be bothered with strategies and pretenses (unless their egoic tendencies have been particularly strong). They no longer seem to be in competition with anyone and feel no compulsion to prove themselves. Consequently, they are often more kind and understanding with others. Younger people may look at this state as something to be avoided, a kind of netherworld of the half dead. But in the lived experience of a relaxed and genuine self, there is such contentment that the roller coaster of the inauthentic self with its fear and striving seems a distant memory from a difficult time.

We need not wait until old age to come to this genuine sense of self. We can fall in love with that feeling right now and enjoy it until the end of our days. We can skip over the part where we spend several decades scurrying around in service to endless demands of obsessive thoughts until we are too exhausted to continue. Life is too rich to spend lost in such thoughts. Yes, we may know, as the Chinese say, the ten thousand joys and the ten thousand sorrows. At one moment we are on bended knees and at another we are soaring in the heavens. Yet in awakened awareness, these will only throw into greater relief the abiding presence, our own genuine self, shining through it all.

the price of compromise

"What does it profit a man
To gain the world and lose his soul?"

—JESUS

One night in a residential retreat in the wilds of Oregon, I was speaking about the importance of honesty in relationships when a woman in the front row raised her hand. I had known this woman for only a short while at this point, and although I felt she had a strong love of dharma, I also sensed her to be burdened by private demons. Her face looked troubled and she walked as if invisible weight pressed on her. So it was not surprising when she said, "For two years I have been deceiving someone I love very much."

I guessed at what seemed a likely scenario and asked, "Are you having an affair?"

"Yes," she whispered with bowed head. "And I fear that if my husband finds out I will lose everything I love."

The crowd of nearly one hundred participants sat in total silence, indeed seemed not to even exist, as the woman and I continued our conversation.

"Well," I said, looking at her anguished face, "what do you have now? What is the lie costing you? As you no doubt know, the stress is not only in the big lie of the affair itself because the big lie also requires a thousand small lies every day. And each of those small lies chips away at your soul. Whatever you are getting from this situation, the cost is more than the gain."

The woman nodded knowingly. "What should I do?" she asked.

Although I rarely give specific advice to people about what changes to make in their lives and would not necessarily respond this way in all circumstances, words poured out in her particular case. "The first thing you have to do is tell the truth."

The woman sat silently for an eternal moment and said simply, "Yes, that is what I have to do." And then a wonderful thing occurred. The strain of her compromise lifted from her face and was replaced by the peace of integrity. At that moment I knew that she had returned home to herself. Through tears of relief she asked if she could leave the hall right then and there to go to her husband and tell him the truth. Although this would mean that she would be driving out of a wilderness area late into the night, it seemed the perfect thing for her to do. As she hugged me goodbye in front of the spellbound crowd, I whispered in her ear, "Whatever happens, you will walk in freedom." She practically skipped out of the room.

Two days later she came back to the retreat, beaming. In our evening session I called on her to tell us what had happened as we were all, of course, dying to know. After leaving us those few days prior, she had arrived home to the surprise of her husband and had told him the whole story of her affair. He was so hurt and angry that they postponed further conversation on the subject until the next morning. The next day, however, her husband got up and went out on his motorcycle for many hours. All the while, the woman thought that the world she had known, with loving husband, children, in-laws, and relatives, would end. Although she felt tremendous sorrow at this prospect, she also felt a deep calm. However, when her husband returned, he said that he wanted to keep their marriage together and that he loved her very much. He said that it would take time for this hurt to heal but that they would get through it. She in turn gave him her promise to end the affair. After a day or so, her husband suggested that she return to finish the retreat.

The fact that the husband and wife stayed together makes for a happy ending to this story. But for me, the happy ending was the moment the woman knew that she was going to tell the truth. At that moment she was home free. Even if her husband had thrown her out on the street, she would have been better off than in continuing to live a life of deceiving the people she loved.

For anyone with the slightest sense of empathy or goodness, perpetrating a lie is often more painful than being lied to. Even when you think you are "getting away with" a lie, *you* are the one left living with the deception. As in the children's card game, it is the proverbial Old Maid you get stuck with. And though it may be your own little secret, each time you look at your cards, the Old Maid's face seems to eclipse all the others. Like this, dishonesty in our heart begins to loom large in our awareness. Any pursuit that requires manipulation, lying, or misrepresenting the truth in even subtle ways disturbs the very essence of our being.

When we are true to ourselves, we live in peace, a state

of grace not dependent on circumstance. In awakened awareness we know that there is nothing that can tempt us into compromise because there is nothing that is worth more than peace. I continue to be surprised by what people will trade for peace of mind. People deceive their loved ones, cheat their friends or business acquaintances, connive to destroy another's reputation, or embellish their own personal histories to impress others—all to try to fill some void in themselves. But no matter how great the apparent riches or experiences they derive from these rips in integrity, these must seem like empty trinkets and hollow memories in quiet moments when one cannot deny the cost of the compromise.

Some of us have to make this discovery many times as greed, lust, ambition, or fear get the best of us, and we try once again to "get away with it." We tell a lie, we dissemble, we mislead. But the clear intelligence natters and wriggles in the background until we rectify what is not aligned with truth. We often look back at the mess created by our lies and say, "What was I thinking?" We can see in hindsight that whatever it was that we got from the lie—the affair, the credit for someone else's work, the extra money—it was not worth it. Someone found out; that someone was oneself.

There are those who, throughout history and to this day, will sacrifice everything for truth and freedom. Consider Rembrandt. In his late twenties he was one of the most successful portrait painters in Holland, but he stopped his lucrative work when he could no longer bear to paint sweet and flattering portraits of the rich. He lived out his days in poverty and obscurity in a ghetto in Amsterdam, painting his greatest masterpieces.

Or consider Martin Luther King, Jr. Although he was accustomed to death threats during his years as a civil rights leader, he knew that his days were truly numbered when he began to speak out against U.S. involvement in Vietnam. Despite the warnings of all those closest to him, he continued to express his views on Vietnam, and he seemed to know that he would have to die for it. In the last months of his life, he alluded many times to the possibility of his imminent death. On the very eve of his assassination, he delivered an impassioned sermon to a congregation in Memphis, Tennessee, in which he said that he had been to the mountaintop and had seen the promised land. "I may not get there with you," he prophetically announced. "But I want you to know tonight, that we as a people will get to the promised land."

To live in integrity, in integral wholeness, may cost your friendships, your worldly possessions, your position, or your name. It may even cost your life. But these are lesser sacrifices than losing one's soul.

simplicity of intention

"In complication there is falsehood."

—H. W. L. POONJAJI

Another aspect of genuineness is that of having no complicated agendas. Genuineness in awakened awareness oper-
ates from a clear and simple motivation, that motivation
being to give rather than to get. It allows one to speak and
act from a quietness of heart rather than from the internal
chatter that usually accompanies selfish motivations. In fact,
it is a good test to notice how much noise is in the mind
when engaging in any activity. The more rumination about
the situation (which usually has as its subtext, "How will
this affect *me?*" or "What will they think of *me?*"), the further astray we are from clear intention. Consider a mother
when her baby cries. Without a lot of mental chatter, the
mother feeds the baby. Her intention to serve is uncompli-
cated. Just so, we can offer our acts in the world and in our
relationships without manipulation.

Having no agenda puts others at ease in our presence.
Conversely, when we secretly want something from another there is an underlying tension. This wanting comes
from thinking that something is missing in us and that ex-
tracting the missing something from another can alleviate
that feeling. It requires objectifying others as though they

are slot machines that will deliver a treasure if the right lever is pulled. When we are seeing others in this way, our hearts are inevitably closed because we cannot feel empathy for people while simultaneously seeking to exploit them.

Having an agenda with someone also lies in fixation on the future. It prohibits being present with others and letting things unfold in a natural way, because someone with an agenda seeks to influence the unfolding of events toward his or her own future goal. In simple presence with another, there is no goal and no future. There is only the ever surprising journey in *now,* taking you and your companion where it will. It is akin to listening to music. Enjoying a piece of music does not depend on getting to the end of the song.

A simple and clear intention comes from sincerity of heart. As we become more attuned to the feeling of pure presence, we encounter a joy that is content with simplicity in all forms. We become more averse to complicated motivations because they disturb our essential peace. This doesn't necessarily mean that we go off to live in a cave or sell all of our possessions in order to simplify our lives. Some people's temperaments are at peace while in motion and in handling many details. But there can be stillness or quietness in the center of one's being even while engaged in many activities and details. Their motivations may be simple though their actions are complex.

The quietness of heart in clear intention also fosters flashes of inspiration. When we are sincere and true in our motivations, intuition is heightened and we are more receptive to electrifying impulses of genius. Take, for example, Mahatma Gandhi. His stated motivation throughout his life was to serve God, and to that end he implemented brilliantly simple strategies.

The idea for the Salt Satyagraha, also known as the Salt March, came to Gandhi in a dream. This was at a time in the history of the Indian independence movement when tensions were at a boiling point with the British. Among their many restrictions, the British had forbidden Indians from producing their own salt. Instead, Indians had to purchase this most basic and abundant commodity from the British monopoly that controlled it. Challenging this injustice, Gandhi organized a march of some two hundred and forty miles to the coastal town of Dandi, where salt piles accumulated freely on the beach. He started out his march with seventy-eight members of his ashram, and by the time they reached the coast, several thousand others had joined them. When they arrived at the shore, Gandhi went directly to the salt piles, picked up a pinch of salt, and held it over his head. With this simple gesture, the colonialism of hundreds of years began to crumble. Despite reprisals over the next months, people all over India began buying the contraband salt at a price higher than that sold by the British.

In awakened awareness, our motivation for service becomes simple. There is nothing much to do here except love each other and be of help. People usually know when they are in the presence of someone motivated simply by love, and they respond with trust and support. It is said that Gandhi brought out the best in people who worked with him. Perhaps his own simplicity of heart enabled him to see what was simple and true in others. When we live in that kind of straightforwardness, it transforms our perception of those around us. We are able to see their basic goodness even if they themselves are lost in neuroses or complicated dramas. And our willingness to simply see that goodness can also transform what they are seeing about themselves.

true humility

*"My obligation is this:
To be transparent."*

—PABLO NERUDA

Almost everyone who knows my niece Alicia considers her to be somewhat of an angel. She just came into the world that way. Unpretentious and kind, she has throughout her life seemed unaware of the effect she has on people. One night at dinner, when Alicia was about eight years old, her older sister Bridget told our family that during the day a fight had broken out in the school lunchroom over whose turn it was to sit next to Alicia. Slightly embarrassed, Alicia, sitting next to me at the dinner table, leaned over and whispered, "I don't know why. I'm not nobody."

Of course, that is exactly *why*. She is imbued with the natural humility that comes with genuineness, and being with her gives others permission to be genuine as well. It offers that rare gift of fearlessness, the feeling that in this person's company you need not fear being yourself. In fact, awakened awareness knows that we need never fear being ourselves. It is inauthenticity that creates problems.

We all know the discomfort of being with someone of pretense. There is a story about a famous general who wishes to visit a renowned Zen master. He arrives at the master's temple and presents his card, announcing himself to the secretary as Anzai-san, supreme commander and general of the imperial army. After consulting with the Zen master, the secretary returns and says with some trepidation, "The master said he has no business with you." The general nods silently and, being a wise man, scratches off all titles from his card, leaving only his given name, Anzai-san. "Please take this card back to the master," the general requested. "Ah, Anzai-san," exclaims the Zen master on seeing the revised card. "I would love to meet this man!"

Pretension comes in all guises. One dangerous area, for example, is in the form of spiritual teachers or gurus who have what in Zen is called "the stink of enlightenment." These are people who claim some kind of perfection (or they claim an enlightenment that rationalizes their apparent imperfections), and they are often worshipped and coddled as a result. They usually enjoy great riches and have servants for their every need. It seems the greater their pretensions, the larger their following, as so many people want to believe in something more exalted than themselves.

But for many of us there is something repellent about piety. Give me the fool any day. Didn't we love the class clown, the silly one? Didn't he or she somehow tell the truth more than any preacher ever did? When we take a good look at ourselves through therapy, contemplative practices, or self-inquiry, we usually find any pretense to piety particularly absurd. As Trungpa Rinpoche said, "Meditation is one insult after another." Nevertheless, authenticity doesn't mean indulging base desires, fears, and anger as an expression of being real. Selfish behavior is based in ego fixation, the story of *me,* though it is sometimes rationalized as authenticity.

It takes heart bravery to be truly authentic, a willingness to be sometimes misunderstood or rejected, or to seem foolish. In fact, the word "courage" comes from *coeur,* French for "heart." Yet though there are times when our naked authenticity may make us feel vulnerable, we more often know those times when we have spoken the difficult truth or bared our soul and felt the stronger for it.

Our natural intelligence knows that we need not fear being ourselves and that problems more often come with inauthenticity. Yet how do we come home to genuineness? We lose our sense of authentic self through fear and suffering. In response to past suffering we develop a false self as a cloak or mask in an attempt to protect our true and tender self that has been hurt. Yet maintaining the false self is actually more difficult and painful than living in the vulnerability of the authentic self. And it is very lonely.

As intelligence wakes up, it clearly sees the difficulty and loneliness of pretense and affectation. Presenting oneself as a *somebody* to the world is wearisome and, ironically, an announcement of insecurity. We can never be at ease if there is a show to be kept up. One needs to distance oneself from others; first, because a pretender wants to appear greater than is the case and, like a good magician, needs some secret props; and second, because if people get too close, they will see the low self-esteem that is driving the charade. If found out, the pretender, who hopes with all his heart to be admired, will be pitied instead.

When we feel whole in ourselves there is no need or desire to present ourselves as anything other than simply being. Not being this or that. Just being. Having interviewed the Dalai Lama several times, I have often been asked if I was ever nervous in his company. I always smile at this question because being around the Dalai Lama is one of the most relaxed of all possible experiences. It could be compared to sitting with one's grandmother by a fire. The Dalai Lama puts everyone who meets him at ease because he is so at ease in himself. There are no "phony holy" airs or tense formalities about him and no affected or pious humility. One experiences a man of dignity and forceful personality yet one who is imbued with kindness and playfulness, someone you'd love to bring home to your folks. The truly great person is not one with whom another feels small. The great person is one with whom another feels grand.

True humility does not, however, mean that one goes around with downcast eyes wearing a hair shirt and talking only in whispers. Humility is simply a natural expression of genuineness, of being authentic. In genuineness we know that we are all struggling to various degrees with our conditioned habits of anger, jealousy, and confusion. In genuineness we have compassion for ourselves in our failings, and we therefore find compassion for others more easily as well. We know that these failings do not negate our essential goodness. We therefore accept and present ourselves in total, in our beauty and our shortcomings, as the divine rascals we are.

natural ethics

"Morality is rooted in the purity of our hearts."

—MOHANDAS K. GANDHI

The love that comes with awakened awareness demands a greater sensitivity in behavior than any code of ethics in existence. If our actions come from love, we need no moral codes because we naturally know what hurts and what helps. Love is careful not to cause pain and takes no delight in another's sorrow. Instead, love suffers with someone in pain and would therefore not augment that pain in any way because it increases one's own suffering. Love needs no book of rules, rewards, or threats of punishment to know this. It is effortlessly known in one's heart of hearts. Being genuine requires living there—in one's heart of hearts—and being willing to endure the acute sensitivity of that abode.

In awakened awareness our sense of community naturally expands as we feel increased familiarity with all living beings. When looking into the eyes of a snake, for instance, something in our own reptilian brains might remember itself, even as the more recent parts of our brains recoil. Nevertheless, in this moment of slight recognition, we become more averse to killing the snake. Likewise, whenever we experience familiarity with any other living being—and this

feeling comes more consistently in awakened awareness—
we become averse to doing anything that might harm it.

In our authenticity we are willing to be honest about the
ways our behavior impacts others in the web of life. It becomes impossible to be exclusively concerned about reward
or loss for ourselves or to justify our self-absorption, thinking that it is socially acceptable to look out for Number
One. Instead, in awakened awareness, we are attuned to the
subtlest costs of our existence in the world, and we seek to
lessen those expenses wherever we can. We are genuinely
careful in our behavior toward others, not in compliance to
what we have been taught but in honoring our own authentic goodness which demands that kind of consideration. We
cannot deceive people in order to get what we want because
the discomfort of living with the deceit is greater than the
pleasure obtained. We cannot get by with technically telling
the truth while presenting situations in a way that misleads.

It also becomes impossible to ignore others' lack of basic
necessities while taking more for ourselves. Just as we
wouldn't dream of hoarding so much for ourselves at a
table with all of our close friends and relatives, so that there
was nothing left for our loved ones to eat, we share with
others because we care about them. Our sense of fair play is
not merely a societal custom; it is an impulse born of universal empathy.

Yet in awakened awareness we also realize that life feeds
on life. Our human lives, for example, often demand physi-

cal, emotional, intellectual, and spiritual stimulation. We are hungry animals on many levels—hungry for experience, hungry for things. But we become more watchful of this appetite when we realize how harmful it can be to other living beings. The Buddhist teacher Thich Nhat Hanh points out, for example, that in simply reading the newspaper we are participating in an industry that uses a forest for each major daily paper in the world. When we think of the thousands of daily papers, we may well be staggered by the amount of trees that this one industry alone represents. The book you are now holding also represents a tremendous cost of wood. It is therefore important for the writer and the publisher to bear that ecological cost in mind and to honor the trees used in the book's production as best as they can.

One of our Los Angeles community once worked as an art director in advertising. His biggest contracts came from the tobacco industry. Because he made a lot of money and because he used his own money for wholesome activities and causes, he justified staying in the business for quite some time. But as his own awareness deepened—as his innate intelligence woke up—it became impossible for him to continue in that line of work. He began to inwardly grimace when hearing of lung cancer deaths on the news or seeing acquaintances who were smokers stricken with emphysema. He could no longer separate his participation in advertising from the end result of encouraging people to

smoke. He could not detach himself from the suffering and death that smoking produces. This suffering was no longer happening to some strangers; it was happening to *us*. In quitting this line of work, he has had to adjust to a reduced income, but he is now at peace. His own genuine heart required an alignment between what he felt and what he did.

Sometimes our natural ethics demand that we go against the rules of society or religion. I have always loved the story of the two Zen monks who were about to cross a stream when they noticed a pretty young damsel unable to cross without drenching her kimono. The older of the two monks scooped her up in his arms, crossed the stream, and deposited her on the opposite bank. The two monks continued on their way, but the younger monk was noticeably disturbed. After walking on in silence for a while, the young monk said to the older one, "We monks are not supposed to touch women, especially not young and pretty ones." The older monk replied, "I put the girl down back there. Are *you* still carrying her?"

When our motivation is pure, there is little ripple in the mind even if we have gone against the rules. In fact, in awakened awareness, a lack of mind ripples is a good barometer for being in harmony with one's words and actions. When our mind is agitated and full of regret, it is usually because we have said or done something hurtful to another, something that has gone against the dictates of our basic goodness or has been born of a moment of confusion.

In awakened awareness, regret is not necessarily incurred when breaking society's rules of morality. Regret comes when there has been a lack of kindness. In fact, we need no morality if we have compassion instead.

Societies will always have their rules, and for the most part, they are necessary for the smooth functioning of large populations of people. It is necessary that the rules be studied and adhered to by those who do not yet have a wide opening of their own tender hearts. Otherwise this world would be in even greater mayhem than it is now. But for those whose intelligence is awake, it is possible to rely solely on natural ethics. This is not a study found in books or recited in churches. Natural ethics are written in one's own genuine heart, which knows, in complete simplicity, how to love.

genuine friendship

"When one cries, the other tastes salt."

—SOURCE UNKNOWN

Some years ago I had a conversation with an internationally famous woman singer who was at that time approaching the age of fifty. Sitting at her kitchen table, we talked about the importance of friendship. She told me that because she had become famous at the age of nineteen, she had not learned how to be a friend until later in life. She said that no matter how inconsiderately she behaved in the early years of her rocketing stardom, there was always a line of people waiting to be her new best friend. She grew used to this revolving door of friends until the time when her career began to nose-dive and she was no longer considered a star. She looked around and realized that along the way she had alienated everyone who had ever loved her, those whom she might have counted on when things began to fall apart.

This was a turning point in her life. Never having valued lasting friendship before, she came to realize what a treasure it was and how much she missed it. Because she had been an idol and the focus of so many people's projections, she had believed herself to be special and above all the normal expectations in friendship. But this became a lonely existence filled only with sycophants, until even they departed. She then embarked on a long slow journey involving years of therapy and meditation to learn how to simply be a true friend. Released from her self-importance, she learned to listen to other people's problems and to share in their joys and losses. She opened into the expansiveness that is necessary when we let others take up residence in our hearts.

Listening well and being present for each other is the ground of genuine friendship. It fosters a loyalty that comes

when we have gone through good and hard times with another human being and have rejoiced and suffered with
them along the way. A deep loyalty also gives us permission
to be honest with our friends and to accept their honesty
even when difficult things need to be said. This is made eas-
ier because in genuine friendship, born of awakened awareness, we have each other's best interests at heart. The
honesty, however challenging the topic, is delivered with
kindness.

In genuineness, we are willing to be vulnerable with our
friends—even crazy sometimes—and we rely on their genuineness to accept us as we are. We also rely on trust, that
most important foundation of any relationship, which takes
time to build and a moment to destroy. In understanding its
importance, we are careful not to tell our friends' secrets,
not to barter information about them for gossip, not to
abandon them in a time of need.

There may sometimes exist an undercurrent of jealousy
among friends. While a good friend wouldn't wish harm for
another, he sometimes doesn't celebrate the other's triumphs, especially in fields in which his own talent or success
seems the lesser. But in awakened awareness we delight in
the triumphs of our friends. We become the one to whom
they rush to tell their good news. Our friends' successes simply make us proud to know them and grateful to have their
talent in our lives. We feel toward them as parents might

feel in the success of their children. Their accomplishments enhance our own sense of abundance.

Genuine friendship can also break through barriers of prejudice. A friend of mine told me the story of his mother and her friendship with the writer James Baldwin when Baldwin was a young boy. My friend's mother, whose maiden name was Orilla Miller, worked in a governmental teaching program during the depression. Baldwin was a pupil in the program, and Miss Miller quickly realized how gifted he was. She felt compelled to spend time with him, not only to enhance his education in whatever ways she could but because she genuinely enjoyed his company and his brilliant mind. Over the protest of young Baldwin's minister father, who had a deep distrust of white people, Miss Miller began to take the boy to concerts, movies, museums, and political events. Such a wonderful friendship was forged between the two of them that Baldwin's prejudices about white people, inherited from his father, were forever changed. He would later write that it was "certainly because of her, who arrived in my terrifying life so soon, that I never really managed to hate white people." My friend's mother, a young white woman from the Midwest, had responded from her genuine appreciation of a kindred spirit in the form of a young black boy.

Being a friend in this way comes from being at home in our own true nature which naturally recognizes the commonality of human experience. In our retreats we sometimes engage in an exercise I call "seeing god with God's eyes." The endeavor is simple. People choose a partner from the room, preferably someone they don't personally yet know. A bell rings, each person bows to his or her partner, and they then sit silently looking into each other's eyes for three minutes. At the end of three minutes, the bell rings, the partners bow, and they then find another partner. They do this with three different partners. No words are exchanged; no touching occurs. Only silent gazing, eyes into eyes.

In the quiet of perceiving in this way, one can look at a face and often see there the suffering the person has endured. One can feel her triumphs, the bonds with her children and parents, her twinges of regret. That degree of awakened awareness can even be emotionally overwhelming sometimes, so great is the power of empathy. I have often observed two partners, who, though they have never met before, sit with tears in their eyes over some silent transmission of feeling. Watching this interaction would remind me of a line David Byrne of Talking Heads sang many years ago: "You got a face with a view."

Yet what people mostly report following this exercise is an ineffable *sameness* shining through each being. It is sometimes described as a light that is shining in every face, something akin to the radiance of existence. In awakened awareness we are attuned to this light in ourselves, this radiance of existence, and we feel it in all things. This is what is most genuine about us when all is said and done, and the recognition of it fosters the most genuine meeting with another.

I have recently been visiting a friend in the hospital who is nearing the end of his life. Although he is emaciated from the cancer that has taken over his body, his eyes are more beautiful than ever. All that is left of him is love. We sit together in the warmth of twenty years of friendship and barely speak; yet worlds upon worlds pass between us. Being with him I have the sense that these bodies we so mistakenly think of as ourselves are just arising and dissolving in the presence, the light, the radiance. To actually feel the presence itself as the most genuine taste of this existence seems the greatest of all privileges. Being with my dying friend, I am witnessing the process of yet another body disintegrating into essential particles that will float in this eternal presence. Yet I am also aware of something intangible that remains, the love that is left behind when our bodies are gone.

stop pretending

"One day the sun admitted
I am just a shadow
I wish I could show you
The infinite incandescence."

—HAFIZ, FOURTEENTH-CENTURY PERSIAN POET

Some years ago a young friend of mine, six years old at the time, walked up to me and said the following: "Pretend you are surrounded by a thousand hungry tigers. What would you do?"

I gave it some thought, imagining the scary scenario and feeling more and more tense. Would I pray? Probably not. Would I run? One doesn't outrun tigers. Anxiety began to take hold as I saw in my mind's eye the tigers closing in. I said to my young friend, "Wow, I don't know what I would do. What would *you* do?"

And he replied, "I'd stop pretending."

Sometimes our stories about our lives and problems are the equivalent of visualizing being surrounded by hungry tigers. We paint pictures in imagination and then become frightened by them. We pretend there's something wrong, and we base our unhappiness on the images that exist primarily in our minds.

Occasionally we are popped out of our imagined unhappiness by a real threat. We are sent in for medical tests.
After tensely waiting, during which time the possibility of
dire health problems eclipses all of our petty ones, we get
the results. They are favorable, and we are jubilant. We
vow to "not sweat the small stuff" anymore. We walk out of
the medical facility with a spring in our step, and we notice
the blue sky and fresh air as we hum to ourselves, "What a
Wonderful World."

But as the days or weeks pass, we take for granted our
good health, and we start entertaining thoughts about how
much better life would be if we only had that certain person, experience, or thing that is missing. Although it may
seem that our pictures of the future are happy ones, there is
a flip side to happy fantasies. Whenever we are visualizing a
rosy future, somewhere in our minds there is usually a picture of its opposite. It is this picture, the depressing picture,
that demands an intense imagining of the happy one. Both
pictures rely on each other to be sustained in imagination.

Most of the terrible things we worry about never happen
and, even if they do, are usually not helped by our worrying.
Worrying and telling ourselves stories about what is missing
is a way of denying our genuine well-being in the present. In
addition to the habitual mental conditioning that lures us
away from present awareness, we may also feel somewhat
shy about living in enlivened presence, as though, if we were
to really surrender to it, existence might be too lovely to bear.

There is a story about a young man taking a religious studies exam at Oxford nearly two centuries ago. He and his fellow classmates had been asked to write about the spiritual significance in the miracle of Jesus turning the water to wine. For two hours all the other students busily filled page after page with their thoughts. However, the young man just gazed out of the classroom window through most of the allotted time. Nearing the end of the period, the proctor came over to him and insisted that he start writing or fail the exam. The young man, who happened to be Lord Byron, took up his pen and wrote only one line: "The water met its master and blushed."

Sometimes we blush in the face of our own beauty and goodness. We pretend to be less than we are and to be troubled by things that are not actually happening now but might happen in the future or did happen in the past. We may not feel entirely comfortable being someone who is just fine. This discomfort might stem from our own internal habits of unhappiness or it may be due to the company we keep.

Many times in Dharma Dialogues people have reported situations regarding old friends with whom they no longer want to spend time. Their friendships had been based on sharing problems, and they had come together in the past to lament their miseries. When one of them is no longer interested in imaginary problems, it becomes embarrassing for the lamenting one to keep up the story and tedious for the other one to hear it. I have known people who, in waking up into clear presence, have found themselves no longer part of their old crowd and sometimes no longer involved with their former best friends. While we may feel love for everyone with whom we have shared our journey, it is not necessary that we continue to spend time with those who want to paint frightening pictures in imagination. As the late Ken Keyes said many years ago, "Love is not necessarily a basis for involvement." We can always be available to help our friends, but in awakened awareness it is no longer possible to wallow in lamentation for camaraderie's sake.

In genuineness, we stop pretending that we are unhappy. It is not that we are always ecstatic (although some of us might be) but that we feel a basic well-being in being at all. In forgetfulness we pretend that life is hard and that living is an endurance test. We forget our inner radiance, how much we love, and how much we are loved. Even so, many of us would do anything to extend life. The truth is that we love to be. When we are threatened with not being, it becomes very clear how much we love being. In awakened awareness we remember each day this love of simply being. Although we realize that there are problems in life and that the world can be a dangerous place, we also know how much we delight in it, how fantastic it is to share its wonders with all who celebrate it. We may feel shy in the face of so much beauty but we don't turn away. We don't pretend not to see it. We don't pretend not to be it.

discernment

Later in the afternoon, she rested under a large

shade tree, aware of the many shadows that the

branches and leaves created on the ground around

her, their silhouettes flatly swaying due to wind

blowing high above. Fascinated, she watched this

play of light and shadow as she considered the

polarities of opposites. She knew that opposites are only different points on a spectrum that is whole. She knew that opposites derive from unity. Yet in observing the distinct shapes made by light and shadow, she also noticed that her own ability to appreciate their polarity had increased. All distinctions of this *and* that *appeared in full relief to her even though they were one in their essence. Her discernment now allowed her to clearly distinguish differences while also understanding fundamental unity.*

In past times, this kind of discernment had been hampered by her enchantment with thinking. She had been so preoccupied with thoughts that she could not see what was right before her eyes. Then, too, she had interpreted whatever happened as it related to the quest. Her life's events—her travels, friendships, work, and studies—had been, in her mind, backdrops for the one event of primary importance—the quest. Seeing the world through its relationship to the quest had sometimes weakened her discernment.

Now the quest had fallen away and her perception was resplendently clear. She no longer interpreted anything she saw or felt through hopes of something that might happen in the future or fears that it might not come to be. Because she now felt whole, she did not need reality to be any different than it was, and, therefore, she was able to see more clearly.

The wind picked up suddenly and the shadows began to dance and flicker, their elongated shapes signaling the last hours of the day's light. She stood to feel the sun and wind on her face.

*As she walked toward the river, the caws of a bird blended with
the sound of the rising wind, yet remained its own piercing
music.*

as it is

> *"Within the illusion of separation we think we see an alien
> world with which we have to negotiate. Clear seeing,
> however, celebrates the wonder of oneness, simply as it is."*
> —TONY PARSONS, AUTHOR OF *AS IT IS*

A friend of mine, who is a high-powered film industry ex-
ecutive accustomed to a sixty-hour work week, told me that
some years ago he was with his family at a tropical resort
for a much needed rest. Far away from phones, computers,
fax machines, and e-mail, my friend began to unwind into
island pace. On about the fifth day, he was pushing his
sleeping son in a stroller down a shaded path when he noticed the sounds of birds singing in the trees. He stopped,
and standing quietly with his baby boy in front of him, he
listened intently, hearing them for the first time on his visit
there. He momentarily wondered if they had been singing
like this for the previous five days, but instantly he recognized that, of course, the birds had been there all along.

They obviously hadn't arrived on the island just that day. No, it was he, in effect, who had just shown up.

When we are obsessed with our thoughts, we often cannot clearly see or hear what is right before us. We are blinded and deafened by pictures and voices in our minds that, though they are at variance with reality, seem totally real to us. We then act based solely on imagination.

In its quality of discernment, awakened awareness perceives the actual contents of our experience. Being able to distinguish the types of thoughts and emotions that are arising allows us to determine how much interest we will pay them. Discernment, ultimately, enables us to choose between suffering and peace.

Such clarity is the natural result of a quiet heart and mind. We don't have to intellectually add anything to become discerning. We don't have to strain to see reality; it is shining through us. As Zen Master Suzuki Roshi said, "If your mind is clear, true knowledge is already yours."

The board game of Go consists of a grid on which black and white stones are placed on the intersections, one stone at a time, to control territory. The click of the stones on the board—black, white, black, white—makes for a crisp sound, a perfect auditory counterpart to the visual look of the board itself. Black stones and white ones unambiguously surround each other, clear and crisp as can be.

Yet an unskilled Go player often sees only what he wants to see, that he is surrounding his opponent, when in fact his opponent is surrounding him. It is all there, literally in black and white, but desire often obscures reality. As the Chinese philosopher Chuang Tzu said of an archer overly attached to the goal, "The need to win drains him of power." A great Go master looks realistically at the board and knows exactly who is surrounding whom. Though he has it in mind, he is not fixated on the outcome; he is fully present with what is happening right now.

Awakened awareness sees clearly because it prizes truth above all else, even when seeing the truth means facing hardship. We may experience difficulty, and it may hurt, but there is no denying the truth of the situation.

We can think of people who, unwilling to give up their land or possessions, have refused to leave a dangerous situation, believing that it was not as bad as it seemed or hoping that it would get better. Such decisions have often cost people their lives. But in clear discernment there is no fear of seeing the truth. We may have to give up our homes. We may have to give up everything. But we see the causes and events clearly throughout the process. We can surrender to the truth of the situation because the peace that comes with surrendering to what is occurring in reality mitigates the pain of loss.

Discernment is weakened when we perceive through hopes for a different picture or through resistance to the current scenario. In other words, we have a story of hope or fear that we overlay on reality, and we interpret everything through that story. In confusion, we cannot let ourselves see the truth if it interferes with our story. Awakened awareness, on the other hand, looks at reality, unblinkingly, and tells no story about it. It simply deals with the existing situation, as it is.

The Sufis say, "If you can lose it in a shipwreck, it isn't yours." Since we can lose pretty much everything in a shipwreck, including our bodies, there appears to be nothing to call our own. Yet there is a presence of which we are a part. Not a personal presence, but the presence of existence itself. This cannot be lost in the shipwreck and is our only real wealth. Knowing this, we sense the manifestations of totality as myriad expressions of ourselves, and we feel privileged to watch the grand show coming and going, coming and going.

Clear discernment comes when we feel whole in this way, when we have no need for reality to conform to our fantasies in order for us to be happy. Reality is fantastic enough without our help. And while it is only human and reasonable to have preferences, discerning awareness knows that we win some and lose some and that our inherent peace need not be disturbed in any case. We can have a light relationship to our preferences, the lighter the better, and this promotes clarity in assessing any situation. It also fosters trust. Trust comes from knowing that however things go, we will be fine; we will be in peace in any storm of life. Having a light relationship to preferences allows us to flow with however things are going. Sometimes they go in unexpected ways more beautiful than we ever imagined, more beautiful than we had willed. Sometimes, out of the blue, difficulty presents itself. In either case, we can trust the deep peace of being to guide us through.

There is a story of a Zen master who lived alone on the outskirts of a town. A young unmarried woman in the town had become pregnant and, not wanting to name the real father for fear of reprisals, falsely claimed that the Zen master had fathered the child. The townspeople were outraged and decided to bring the baby to the master to have him take responsibility for raising the child. The Zen master bowed, accepted the baby, and brought the child up with all the love he had. After ten years, the woman recanted her story and came to claim the child. The Zen master quietly bowed and handed the child over to its mother.

In the gladness of beauty and the sadness at loss, there is a continual surrender to the peace that has never been touched by anything, the quiet that has been there through every wild circumstance of our lives. Our experience of life becomes that of acceptance of whatever is unfolding rather than chasing after things or pushing away what is presenting itself. In other words, our experience of life becomes that of surrender to what is. In this surrender, there are no lost opportunities.

Accepting what already is does not imply passivity or an inability to be committed in life. When action is needed, action occurs. One may endeavor to save a rain forest, get married and have children, or go off to a monastery. Whatever happens is seen as the unfolding of events while the attention is at rest in the quiet that is not dependent on any particular event for one's happiness.

When we surrender in this way, we find ourselves just flowing along with life's circumstances. The actual feeling of surrender is sweet in itself, like floating downstream. It doesn't matter whether we are surrendering to the caretaking of a new baby or a dying parent, our internal experience can be that of a force moving through us, handling everything with diamond clarity. Our own desires become merged with this flow and we find ourselves saying yes. Yes to whatever is.

beyond biology

Some years ago I was flying into the island of Molokai, one of the less populated Hawaiian Islands, in an eight-seater plane. Ten minutes from landing, we encountered a rollicking storm of hurricane winds. The young pilots of the small charter airline seemed nervous and barely able to keep the plane steady as they pushed on toward our destination. Every now and then we would get a glimpse of Molokai in a parting of clouds. Mountains surrounded the runway, leaving only one approach. There would not be much room for error, I thought, as the winds hurled the plane about in flashes of lightning and booms of thunder. We aborted our first two attempts at landing, each time making circles in zero visibility near spires of rock shooting into the sky. At any second, I felt the plane might crash and explode into one of them.

Adrenaline shot through my system to the point of nausea. Designed for fight or flight, the hormone was not at all desirable in a situation where one was strapped in a seat. I sat there, experiencing the discomfort of fear chemicals surging through my body along with one burning thought: "I don't want to die like this."

Nevertheless, there was also a strange calm, a witnessing presence throughout the entire ordeal. It was as though the event was happening on two levels: the biological level in which fear and the wish to survive dominated all other concerns, and a second level in which a deeper awareness was peacefully watching the entire show. It is this second level of witnessing awareness that can keep us steady throughout our trials. It is always there. All that is required is to notice it. The biological level of awareness reacts in whatever ways it needs. But awakened awareness keeps the situation in clear focus, a calm influence over the intense physical reaction.

Back on the ground and waiting for luggage, my body felt spent and limp as a rag doll. My emotional body, too, felt exhausted with trails of thoughts about how close a brush with death we had just had. These feelings seemed normal, even healthy. The organism had responded appropriately to a threatening situation. I had no "spiritual" story about it not being okay to have experienced intense fear and a strong preference to live. Fear in the face of physical danger is an innate reflex that helps keep us alive, and preferring to live is natural to every creature. Yet there was a simultaneous awareness that remained perfectly at peace, just noticing the physical and emotional reactions to the flight.

Discerning awareness recognizes the powerful influence of biology on human behavior. From the time we are born, we exhibit responses and reactions that are consistent with people the world over. The fascinating new field of evolutionary psychology, or the study of genetic conditioning on behavior, traces our most deeply ingrained instinctual impulses and connects almost all of them to our capacity to survive and to propagate our genes. In fact, propagation of the genes seems to be the driving force underlying most of what we say, do, and think, according to evolutionary psychology. It sees the brain as a "wet computer" whose circuitry is designed to respond to information in the environment, the primary objective being to stay alive and pass on the genes. In other words, evolutionary psychology sees us as a complex delivery system for genes.

As compelling as this view is (and study of it closes almost every loophole one can imagine), there is plenty of wiggle room for mystery. As Francis Collins, head of the Human Genome Project, said, "We will not understand important things like 'love' by knowing the DNA sequence of homo sapiens."

We might consider, for instance: what is the intelligence animating the DNA? And is there any awareness that is not based strictly on biological imperatives? We could say that awakened awareness is an intelligence that coexists with the DNA program. It therefore is able to witness the biologically induced behaviors, but it is not enslaved to them.

Still, we recognize that the biological program has a huge influence on behavior, and it is foolish to underestimate it. Our basic drives of competition, attraction to beauty or power, self-preservation, anger, and jealousy are genetically based and are common in startlingly similar ways to other primates with whom we share an almost identical genetic make-up. (For example, in the case of chimpanzees, we share over 98 percent of our genes.) I have many times watched wild street monkeys in India displaying familiar human behaviors as though hyped on speed; one minute fighting over food or some minor infraction, the next minute copulating, and the next minute jumping onto a shocked tourist to grab a banana from her hand.

Watching monkeys can be disconcerting, as it is so easy to identify with their selfish primal drives. We humans have social rules of engagement and punishing consequences that deter our acting on similar primal drives, but as we all know, these deterrents don't always work. We sometimes take more than our share, lie when we think it necessary, sleep with our best friend's spouse. We see successful men, alpha males (a term originally used to describe dominant male gorillas), storming through the world taking whatever they want, and we may secretly admire them for being able to do so. We can at least identify with these impulses, as they are part of our own survival and procreative conditioning as well. To deny them is disingenuous. To pretend piety when we know that our biological impulses are basically selfish and, for a large part of our lives, driven by lust is hypocritical. The restless and selfish motivations of monkey mind are quite familiar to every one of us, and humility, not piety, seems the only reasonable response in the face of them.

In clear discernment primal impulses based in biology are easily recognized. Many of these impulses are necessary for survival of the organism. When we are hungry, we eat; when thirsty, we drink; when tired, we sleep, and so on. No more complicated than that. Awakened awareness lets the biological program take care of these survival needs without much interference, just as it does when we sneeze. Not much thought required. In fact, it lets us wholeheartedly be the animals we are in our bodily needs and has no use for gussying up those animal needs with stories or philosophy. It gives the instinctual body full reign to take care of itself, as the instincts are best at doing so.

Discriminating awareness is also alert to the genetic conditioning that can drive self-preservation tendencies into pure selfishness. It is able to see beyond the needs of personal biology while fully including it in a larger context. While discernment knows that it is important to take care of the organism known as *me,* it also cares deeply for other creatures and the environment in which we all live. This caring tends to serve the greatest good, so if personal sacrifice provides something greater for the whole, discerning awareness will choose it. In fact, in clear discernment it doesn't feel like sacrifice. Just as a mother, in a shortage of food, would want to feed her child before herself, discerning awareness naturally prefers serving the greater good.

Sometimes the awareness can become misguided in taking too *little* care of oneself. There are stories of spiritual teachers who paid so little attention to their bodies that they would fail to notice if they were cut and bleeding. There are people who give and give until they collapse. These cases often require that others then become their caregivers. Neglecting to take care of oneself is as much an imbalance as the purely self-centered view of *me first.*

In many teachings, ignoring bodily needs is seen as an exalted state and a sign of spiritual advancement. But that perspective seems antiquated. It comes mostly from cultures that were heavily biased in views of transcendence. They wanted to escape this world in favor of what they imagined to be higher realms. In viewing all worldly life as illusory, they dissociated from their own bodies. In other transcendent traditions, people actually harmed their bodies in attempts to "mortify the flesh in order to free the spirit." They, too, hoped to disassociate from the body and its desires.

In awakened awareness we honor the needs of the body and we delight in the pleasures of it. At the same time, our discerning awareness quietly encompasses a larger view in which its motivations include the well-being of others. This discernment provides a natural equipoise between caring for oneself and caring for others, and it knows when an imbalance occurs. When it is time for the caregiver to rest, he rests. When he is filled with rest and pleasure, he gives it all away again.

no beliefs

> "The great enemy of the truth is very often not the lie—deliberate, contrived, and dishonest—but the myth—persistent, pervasive, and unrealistic."
>
> —JOHN F. KENNEDY

In 1983 I interviewed J. Krishnamurti in New York City on an assignment for *East/West Journal.* As I began a question with the words "Sir, do you believe . . . ?" he stopped me midsentence with upheld hand and said, "I don't believe in anything." On hearing this, I was momentarily taken aback. How was that possible? Most of our worldviews are based on beliefs. But the possibility came immediately into focus. Not only could we live without beliefs, we could live with far greater clarity if we relied solely on direct experience. We would not interpret reality through the dull light of dogma. We know our own experience through having lived it. Knowing the pure experience, without beliefs and interpretations, is all we need for clarity.

We also appreciate those who are willing to speak from direct experience rather than from a system of beliefs. What a difference it makes to listen to someone describe what he has lived and felt rather than hear someone lecture from texts. A palpable authority issues from one who speaks of his life's journey. As Poonjaji would say, "A true teacher gives you only his or her experience; all else are preachers."

Discriminating awareness guides us in knowing the true from the false. We grow up in a certain time and culture, inheriting the myths of that culture, and we often go along without questioning them. But a simple way to test our commitment to these myths is to sincerely ask ourselves: Have I directly experienced this, or have I just heard it many times?

The currently fashionable term "cultural relativism" is often understood to mean that truth is relative to one's cultural conditioning. If your culture thinks that the earth was created ten thousand years ago by the sun god, then that is as true as any other myth, according to the cultural relativists. People in those belief systems think that the discoveries of science are nothing more than the myths of certain cultures. Even when presented with evidence or data culled from many disparate sources, they are unable or unwilling to release their beliefs.

Moral relativism is an even more slippery slope. The custom of female circumcision, still practiced by millions, is often defended on grounds of moral relativism, as are numerous acts of brutality that are sanctioned against humans and other creatures alike. In the case of female circumcision, this barbaric act perpetrated on mostly young girls requires the screaming victims to be forcibly held down as they struggle to avoid mutilation. Massive infection or death can result at worst, a lifelong inability to experience sexual pleasure at least.

While we do not deny a culture's right to practice their beliefs, it is always important to examine whether anyone is being hurt by their practices. Foot binding of women in China came to be seen for the cruel custom that it was; sati, the centuries-old cultural practice for widows in India to immolate themselves on their husband's funeral pyre, was eventually outlawed; and slavery in the civilized world is now unthinkable. These examples and hundreds more like them show that challenging beliefs that cause misery, no matter how customary they are, is the first step toward change.

To those who say that right and wrong are arbitrary values, I offer the words of Seung Sahn, a Korean Zen master: "There is no right and no wrong, but right is right and wrong is wrong." We know right and wrong in our own hearts. Does an action conduce to love and kindness or does it cause pain and suffering?

While certain beliefs clearly stand out as being culturally conditioned, some are more subtle. In awakened awareness, our own discernment carefully separates what is true from what is believed to be true. Not needing to uphold a preconceived idea, discernment willingly applies scientific testing methods to any working hypothesis. Are the results consistent when tested by different experimenters, in different places and times, without prejudice to outcome? Or does the hypothesis rely primarily on interpretations about subjective experiences, such as, for example, someone claiming to remember being Cleopatra in a former life? The pure experience might have been some strong thoughts about and identification with Cleopatra. There may have been a visual scene in one's imagination of tiled rooms or water urns or statues. But to interpret that imagery to mean that one was actually Cleopatra is a leap of fantasy.

People cling to beliefs for comfort. To assuage their fear of the unknown and to attempt to feel some control over their lives, they employ psychics and tarot readers, engage in all kinds of dubious self-help and health practices, chase gurus, or go to UFO conferences to hear tales of people communing with extraterrestrials.

In awakened awareness, there is no desire to bend the laws of nature (and no belief that it is possible to do so).[2] Life, as it is, is miraculous enough. If we pay attention, the miracles are happening before our eyes. The baby takes its first steps, exhibiting that the DNA instructions copied over several hundred thousand generations are in perfect working order. What kind of marvelous intelligence is at work in that feat? If we stopped for a moment to consider the wonders of existence, our own lives a mysterious universe even to ourselves, we would not need to be entertained by magic tricks. We would understand what Walt Whitman meant when he said, "To me, every moment of the day and night is an unspeakably perfect miracle."

Of all kinds of beliefs, those offered by religions are perhaps the most compelling due to their promises of life after death. In fact, the promise of an afterlife seems to be the primary focus in most religions, and many demand tremendous sacrifice and repression in this life for the reward of carrying on pleasantly in the next. I often wonder, however,

---

2. *All efforts by science work within the laws of nature. Even the manipulation of genes in cloning, ethical questions aside, is based on understanding these laws and working within them.*

why many people who claim to believe in a glorious after-life are not more anxious to get there. One would think they would be exiting in droves to escape the vicissitudes of this world if they knew for certain they were going to meet their maker, be reunited with their dearly departed loved ones, and live in heavenly bliss. Perhaps, as it was for me when I used to entertain such hopeful thoughts, there is a nagging doubt. This doubt is a seed of discernment. It knows that it simply doesn't know what happens after death.

We have been handed down belief systems of specula-tion on the origins and purposes of the cosmos from primi-tive societies of people who did not know the earth was round or that germs existed. They generally lived short lives, were mostly uneducated, and traveled very little. They believed in ghosts, spells, and hundreds of other su-perstitions. To think that these people would have had some special knowledge about what happens after death that is now inaccessible to us in modern times defies reason. That a myth is old doesn't make it true.

Hoping *to be* after the death of the body clouds our dis-criminating awareness. For many, it is more comforting to cling to beliefs about an afterlife in heaven or a better re-birth on earth than to accept life and death as a mystery. Discerning awareness, however, is not concerned with the loss of comfort associated with belief or myth. Comfort that relies on assumptions about the future is imaginary.

We don't need a belief system to feel the aliveness or passion of existence right now. And this existence becomes all the more valuable when we have no assumption about its continuation. We no longer squander the wealth of time that we actually have for the promise of living in some other time. We are instead immersed in the wondrous present. Our intelligence becomes white-hot in its ability to challenge any of our own beliefs that may continue to arise, and consequently, we live in a state of perpetual innocence.

things change

> "Change alone is unchanging."
>
> —HERACLITUS

You go to your old hometown and can't find your way around anymore because the streets have changed. You go to the field where, as a kid, you used to play ball, and there is now a Wal-Mart there. You look through your address book and see the names of several friends who have died. You catch a glimpse of yourself in a store window and wonder who that older person is who looks so much like you. Singer/songwriter Carly Simon once described such a glimpse of herself as "seeing a young woman looking older for the part."

Fossils of seashells and marine animals are sometimes found high in the Himalayan rock, an indication that it was once the bottom of the sea. We are reminded of impermanence simply by looking at the night sky. Some of the stars we think we see no longer exist. All that is left of them is the light that bounced from them and is now traveling through space. In some ways, we could think of ourselves as leaving nothing much behind but the light that bounces from us. Sometimes, when we are very quiet, we might sense it lighting everything.

"Time is a jet plane; it moves too fast. Ah, but what a shame that all we've shared can't last." Bob Dylan's words sum up the poignancy inherent in our human predicament. We will be separated from all that we love, all that we hold dear. However, even in the sadness of loss, awakened awareness doesn't clutch too tightly to what it loves because it knows that it is pointless to do so. While we honor and deeply feel the sadness, we need not compound it by resisting one of the most fundamental of truths: everything passes. My teacher once said, "The wise are attracted by the eternal while the foolish pursue the transient and are thus bludgeoned by time."

Recently I saw a billionaire business mogul interviewed on television. At the time of the interview the man was in his mid-seventies, excitedly describing to the interviewer his accomplishments as well as his long-range plans for projects spanning the next quarter century. The interviewer, quite boldly I thought, asked him if he thought he might miss seeing some of those dreams come true, given his age. The man looked at the interviewer in incredulity. With some disdain he answered that he fully planned to oversee those projects and had no intention of dying any time soon.

I couldn't imagine how anyone of average intelligence could get to be his age and not have noticed the one-pointed trajectory of bodily disintegration, the proverbial "arrow of time." It is a testament to the power of denial. Perhaps this denial had helped the billionaire in building his empire. Maybe he had never been distracted from the building task by self-reflections on mortality or who-am-I, what-is-this-thing-called-life questions. Perhaps the urge to build an empire is in itself an attempt to challenge the law of impermanence. Hoping to leave something "permanent" behind is a way to feel an extension of oneself in time, if only through name. But posthumously having one's name on a few buildings, plazas, museums, street signs, or books is hardly an experience of immortality. And our world is becoming more and more littered with the artifacts of humans wanting to leave their mark on it. As Alan Watts once observed on the ego's dedication to its own continuation: "To feel [that] life is meaningless unless 'I' can be permanent is like having desperately fallen in love with an inch."

"Perfect activity leaves no trace." I am reminded of these Taoist words when I think of my friend Helen Nearing whose husband Scott had just died when I met her in 1983.

Helen and Scott were some of the original back-to-the-land pioneers in the U.S., moving first to Vermont in 1932 and, when Vermont became too developed for them, to Maine in 1952. Living entirely off the grid, hand-building their homes from stones found on their land, and growing their own food, they exemplified what it means to tread lightly on the earth.

Beginning in the 1950s, the Nearings wrote a number of books, including their classic *Living the Good Life*. In them they described a commitment to self-sufficiency, hard work, simplicity, and a love of learning. They were also lifelong proponents of social and environmental causes. When, at the age of one hundred, Scott fell sick and could no longer work, he decided to fast to the end. Helen told me that Scott died as he had lived, in full consciousness and consideration of the earth, asking for the simplest of cremation arrangements and requesting that his ashes be scattered on their land. After more than fifty years together, Helen said that being present at his death was as gentle as watching a leaf fall from a tree.

Change is part of the natural rhythm of life, but our culture has begun to confuse change with speed. We overlook the deeper changes of life and are instead continually adjusting to ever increasing velocities of speed in nearly all activities. As we adjust to new speeds, we increase our expectations for the current speed, or for acceleration. If you are old enough, you will remember dialing rotary phones or getting up to change the channels on the television, neither of which seemed a hardship at the time. In today's world, few would have the patience required for these simple activities. Even those of us who grew up with those technologies would find them almost unbearably slow and tedious because our brains now expect those functions to be much faster.

Many television programs in the fifties and sixties aired scenes that lasted up to fifteen minutes with no camera changes. Now we are used to images changing every few seconds, sometimes so fast that they are only subliminally recorded in our minds. Instant access to information, instant communication, instant ordering of products, instant transfer of funds; we value and expect speed, and we measure time in nanoseconds.

We have witnessed significant changes in the past century, more than in any other time in history. But much of what we experience as change in our lives has been, in fact, an adjustment to speed. We have lost touch with the natural and slower tempos of life, and consequently we have become more resistant to real life changes.

Nowhere is that resistance more pronounced than in our relationship to aging. It has seemingly become unfashionable to look or be old. Perhaps one of the reasons we desperately resist aging is that our culture no longer values the wisdom that comes with age. We live in a youth-obsessed society in part because we value speed, and the young are better at speed. We have ads showing children helping their grandparents learn to use computer programs, with captions that say, "It's so easy, even an older person can learn it." Of course, the grandfather can learn it, but it takes longer. The grandfather may have a thing or two to teach as well—the hard-won lessons that come only with time. He may not have a lot of speed, but he is likely to know a great deal about change. Sadly, older people often feel that no one is really interested in them because they are *old*. And so there is societal pressure to appear not to be aging, for fear of being seen as useless. Our attempts to appear younger are not necessarily for the pleasure of looking at ourselves in the mirror or dazzling new suitors, but to continue to be included in life.

While it makes sense to take the best care of ourselves as possible—to try to stay physically strong and mentally alert—in awakened awareness there is a graceful recognition of the aging process. I loved the sight of Helen Nearing, in her eighties when I last saw her, about seven years before she died. With her wizened, weathered face, intelligent eyes, and wiry strong body, she was an inspiration for growing old with dignity. In discerning awareness there is a great respect for the elders of our society and for the wisdom that comes with age. (I have always secretly thought that grandmothers, not middle-aged men, should rule the world.)

Awakened awareness is always mindful of the ever-present fact of impermanence and therefore treasures the tender beauties of life. Whether seeing a shower of shooting stars on a summer night or the veins in the hands of your parent, we are aware of the continual passing of all phenomena. Nearly thirty years ago, at the end of a silent Buddhist retreat, a young man put a note on my meditation cushion that said, "Would you like to join me to watch a totally original sunset?" I realized in a flash that his question contained the bittersweet truth. A sunset is a one-time event, each one a first and last—just like each passing flicker of our lives.

waiting for the miracle

"Baby, I've been waiting
I've been waiting night and day
I didn't see the time
And I waited half my life away
There were lots of invitations
And I know you sent me some
But I was waiting for the miracle
For the miracle to come"

—LEONARD COHEN, "WAITING FOR THE MIRACLE,"
FROM THE ALBUM *THE FUTURE*

We wait and wait. We look forward to the time that we will start living our *real* lives. We wait for all kinds of hopeful events, ignoring the rich taste of *now* in favor of the blanched experience of fantasy. We think that we will finally be happy when we find the perfect spouse or lover, or we get rid of the one we have, or when we start a new career, make more money, or have children, or the children leave home, or we find a spiritual teacher, or we take that trip around the world. We dream about what might be or might have been, but as the old Everly Brothers song said, "Only trouble is, gee wiz, I'm dreamin' my life away."

We postpone in myriad ways living in the true miracle—the miracle of here and now. The great teacher Nisargadatta Maharaj said, "It is reality that makes the present so vital, so different from past and future, which are merely mental." Reality, here and now, has a vitality to which no fantasy can compare.

Discerning intelligence knows that happiness as a concept relates to the future. Similarly unhappiness is an idea. To test this, make a simple experiment. When you are experiencing suffering—mental suffering—notice that your attention is fixed on an image or a series of thoughts, a story. Notice how the thoughts and images are dependent on a central idea, the idea of somebody—that is, *me*—and the problem. The suffering exists in the story, not in reality. What is the suffering without the idea of me and the problem?

When we release the image of the central character on whom the problems depend, the problems naturally disappear. The Buddha, upon awakening, is said to have remarked, "O, housebuilder, I have seen you; your ridge pole[3] is broken." Seeing through the illusion of the central character breaks the ridge pole of the entire house of suffering.

Awakened awareness simply sees the unfolding of totality as a flow of life, rather than a subject/object dichotomy of me and the object of my desire or fear. There can be enjoyment and profound love of whatever beauty comes along in that flow without hoping that it keeps happening in the future. So often we are stymied from enjoying present beauty because we fear that it will end. We resist giving ourselves to it because we don't want to be hurt when it's gone, preferring instead to simply fantasize about happy experiences. Though not as much fun, at least we can control the fantasies.

Discerning awareness, on the other hand, does not use fantasy life as a substitute for reality. Real life provides all the fascination required. Even if nothing much is happening, there is a current of joy and appreciation bubbling along. In our retreats people become so happy and unresisting to the tender feelings that come with that happiness that it borders on being unbearable. Tears flow from just quietly watching a grasshopper or a sunset or a person bending to tie his shoelaces. What accounts for such shifts in perception when all that has occurred is that people have become

---

3. *A ridge pole is the main beam that attaches all other rafters to the roof of a house.*

quiet and attuned to their own presence? What makes circumstances that might seem boring to many so full of happiness for some?

Fritz Perls, the founder of Gestalt therapy, once remarked, "Boredom is lack of attention." Like a cranky distant relative who is never satisfied, boredom can say that peace is not enough, that we will be happier when there is more excitement. So we wait in a state of "if only" for the miracle to come, and we miss the miracle of life that is happening right now. In awakened awareness, every moment we are experiencing is rich, no matter how devoid of activity or entertainment. There might be times in one's life, for instance, that may seem fallow. On the surface it may appear that nothing is happening. But if we are attuned to the depths of our existence, those times could be metaphorically experienced as winter. Although it looks as though life is dormant on the surface, there is a powerful force of energy going on beneath. We can feel this powerful presence of life—creative, destructive, and wondrous—as we are its own expression. We might burst out of such a winter-of-the-soul period like the arrival of spring, with all kinds of creative ideas and insights. Even if that is not to be, we can bask in the deep peace of life's expression in quietude. Every moment that we are aware of the gift of simply being, with or without activity, is well lived.

Ludwig Wittgenstein said, "If we take eternity to mean not infinite temporal duration but timelessness, then eternal life belongs to those who live in the present." Actually, we all live only in the present. It is simply a matter of recognizing the fact. It is always now. There is no experience of time other than now—ever. The future never comes. As I write these words, it is now. As you read them, it is now. All thoughts about past and future occur only in the present. You cannot take one toe step out of it, despite your most fervent thoughts about any other time.

When we live in that knowing, in present awareness, we acclimate to a current of aliveness that is far preferable to fantasies about the future or memories of the past. Thinking about time falls away and our lives flow along in wakeful presence. My teacher used to say that "death is simply when the next breath does not come." Until then we are living in the eternal *now*. Always now.

d e l i g h t

She was walking on a path by the river when she

heard a plop. Looking in the direction of the

sound, which came from the vicinity of her feet,

she saw a frog just a few inches from her, hopping

in her direction. They went on together for a few

steps like this when she deliberately slowed her

pace. The frog slowed as well. She walked faster, and the frog hopped faster, too. She began to laugh so hard that she soon had to sit down. And the frog also sat.

As delightful as the frog was, she knew that her delight came from a deeper well, an innate delight that was not bound to a particular experience. It was as if it was always there, a current of joy flowing through her, waiting for an excuse to spring out. Feelings and memories from childhood flooded her awareness like a multitude of fireflies as she basked in the amusement with the frog, her current of joy particularly strong. She felt, once again, an inexplicable excitement about being alive, and simple things were enormously interesting, pleasurable, and funny.

She reflected on the sadness of existence as well, to see if the current of joy could withstand it. But there it was, a quiet inner happiness, despite everything. She was in love with life, with the very fact of it, the incomprehensible event of existence. She felt as if she were quietly celebrating the day, her delight being the natural response to the gift of life. She knew that nothing was needed for this celebration, not even the frog. Meanwhile, he had perhaps grown impatient with her musings. As she continued to sit, the frog hopped slowly toward the river.

innocence

"Except ye become as little children
Ye shall not enter the kingdom of heaven."

—JESUS

On the last day of one of our silent retreats a man spoke about the parting words he had heard from his girlfriend before leaving her the week before. "Now, don't you go and fall in love with someone there," she told him. The man looked around at the group of sixty and said, "How am I going to explain that I fell in love with *everyone*?" I assured him that his girlfriend probably wouldn't mind that as much.

One of the great gifts of my life comes from witnessing what happens in silent retreats. Participants, many of them strangers to each other, come together and, with the exception of two hour-long group sessions per day, are silent for a week. They are given no spiritual practice or instructions but are encouraged instead to rest as much as needed and to notice throughout the day the clear awareness to which no thought ever sticks.

Day by day, joyousness and surprising bursts of energy infect the participants as they feel the naturalness of being awake and sharing companionship without the stories and ego presentations that usually make up society. People will frequently describe feelings that are familiar from child-hood such as waking up in the day and feeling excited for no particular reason. We refer to this as causeless joy or the pure joy of existence. It is sometimes experienced as a current that flows inside, like champagne bubbles of well-being.

The feeling of well-being emerges from our natural condition of innocence. In awakened awareness, the clear perception through which we regard the world is renewed each moment. We are no longer mentally dragging around the hardened crust of history about ourselves or having to wear the weighty armoring of self-importance.

I once spent a couple days on the island of Lanai in Hawaii at an exclusive resort that often attracts guests who are titans of industry. One day I was walking on a path down to the ocean and an older man passed me. I immedi-ately sensed an imperious attitude in his purposeful march and his cheerless determined face that seemed carved out of stone. We looked each other in the eye, and a chill wind blew through my soul. I was reminded once again of the burden of thinking of oneself as somebody in the world, someone with power over others. I felt compassion for the man because, despite whatever wealth he had accumulated, I sensed only his impoverishment at missing what I con-sider the best of life. If one is not in touch with one's inno-cence, there is no heaven to be found, even in the most beautiful places on earth.

The most consistent characteristic of awakened teachers and people I have met is a childlike nature. They laugh, cry, twinkle, and joke, all with a spontaneity born of freedom. Their faces are fluid and reflect a timeless sweetness, even into old age. Poonjaji, a model of dignity into his eighties, could be at times downright goofy—and we loved it. He also exhibited a free-flowing range of emotions. On my first visit to meet him I noticed that almost every day he would laugh and cry several times during gatherings with students. Sometimes his tears would come from the happiness of seeing a person release a long held burden; sometimes he would cry with someone who had suffered a loss. As with a child, feelings would pass through him and be gone as quickly as they had come, leaving no lingering mood behind.

We all love the innocence we see in children. We delight in watching them learn new things and play in wild abandon. We love to hear their questions and reflections about the world because they spring from original awareness and the brilliance that obtains. We wistfully watch them sleeping and remember that feeling of perfect peace. We delight in the company of children because they remind us of our own innocence.

But in awakened awareness, innocence is no longer the special province of children. We, too, delight in learning new things and playing in abandon; our original awareness questions and reflects in brilliance; and we, too, sleep in deep peace. Innocence is a condition not dependent on age but on attitude. It lives in continual surprise, not knowing how things are supposed to go, not needing them to go a certain way.

When I was a child growing up in Virginia, my parents would, on a regular basis, tell my brother Bob and me to get in the car. We would rarely be told where we were going. We might end up at the grocery store or in Florida. Each journey in the car was a wondrous adventure because we could turn up just about anywhere. We not only had no clue about where we were going, we had no notion that our destination was something of which we should be informed. We were truly just along for the ride.

In awakened awareness, we rediscover our innocence. The intelligence sees that, despite the memories of many years, there is yet a presence that has never been written upon in memory and exists only and always now. We are once again along for the ride, and life itself becomes a wondrous adventure as we let it take us rather than chase it down. This doesn't mean that we passively lie around until someone says, "Go get in the car." It simply means that we feel and move through the world with hearts of innocence. Wherever fate leads—in passion or quiet—an innocent heart makes the journey heavenly. Where we end up or what we see along the way is of less consequence.

pervasive beauty

"May you walk in beauty."

—NAVAHO BLESSING

In awakened awareness, seeing beauty results from one's perception and not necessarily from the thing perceived. What we often describe as beautiful is merely a conditioned interpretation that is entrained to see one thing as beautiful and another as revolting. Awakened awareness, however, overrides this conditioning and is able to see beauty in the most unlikely of places because it sees the universal essence of things.

Some years ago, I was in India to visit Poonjaji when a dramatic shift in my perception occurred. I had become, over many trips during the previous twenty years, more and more allergic to India. By that I mean I had developed such revulsion for the sights, smells, and sounds that accost one's senses every day there that I went around with a slight feeling of nausea. Nevertheless, India continued to draw me because of its rich spiritual heritage and the great teachers who lived there. I also enjoyed being occasionally unplugged from the hectic pace of Western life, and, in the old days at least, India provided a feeling of stepping into the colonial past the moment I emerged from the plane onto the subcontinent. But I had long ago lost all romantic notions about much of India and instead noticed its disease, pollution, poverty, and superstition. It seemed after a while that my eye fell upon ugliness at nearly every turn.

Being with Poonjaji changed all of that. I began to sense the presence of the life force in myself and, soon, in everything around me. While I was showering one day, the bath tiles came alive as I imagined, could almost feel, their subatomic particles swirling within. When walking, I no longer experienced myself as a separate body but as a movement in and through an all-encompassing landscape. This perception in turn produced feelings of warmth and appreciation for every strange, wonderful, or ordinary thing I chanced upon. Now, wherever my eye landed, my heart was lit up by the indwelling presence it recognized there. The wart hogs eating garbage on the side of the road became beautiful to me because I could feel my own essence and sense that same essence in them. They and I, embodying different forms, were just part of the unbounded panorama of existence.

In Zen they say, "When you wake up, the whole world wakes up." One's awakened awareness recognizes its own nature in everything, seeing its source as the source of all. One then perceives in love and wholeness, experiencing beauty not merely in certain objects, people, or places but as an awakened heart intelligence at one with its world.

So often our definition and appreciation of beauty comes from a limited awareness. Sure, we can see beauty in the

creamy pink cheeks and shining eyes of a child, in the purple and red glow of sunrise over a snowy field, or in the languid grace of a gorgeous woman. Identifying these as beautiful requires no special intelligence. Our genes and cultural conditioning do that work for us. We easily respond to typical triggers of instinct and what we have been taught to define as beauty.

But in awakened awareness the experience of beauty is not about how a person, place, or thing looks; it is about how the one who is looking *feels.* We are able to see beauty even in what our instincts or cultural conditioning define as horrid. This is not in a Pollyanna sense of seeing a silver lining in every cloud or telling stories that deny the horrid. The horrid is also seen and noted in awakened awareness but is accepted as part of the whole. As a human animal we may move away from an unpleasant smell, but we need not experience the smell as an alien force, separate from totality. Rumi said, "Imagine the delight of walking on a noisy street and *being* the noise." In awakened awareness we are not mentally carving up the world into what should be included or not. We sense the world as a vast extension of ourselves. We belong to it and it belongs to us. Imagine the delight.

The beauty that we experience in outward manifestation is a direct reflection of the beauty of our internal reality. Have you ever noticed how someone you love or one who has simply been kind to you may suddenly look beautiful

even though you might have once considered that same face to be plain? What was it that changed? In awakened awareness we are not solely dependent on visual stimulation to experience beauty because we recognize that the greatest conduit for the experience of beauty is love. When we love, we see beauty; we speak in beauty; we walk in beauty. In love, we are beauty itself.

There is a story told by the late Japanese potter Hiroshi Eguchi of a visit to his pottery store in Nagasaki by Helen Keller and her teacher Anne Sullivan in 1948. Blind and deaf since birth, Keller had by that time spent more than sixty years in a relentless love of learning and discovery of beauty. The potter Eguchi had seen his city devastated by the atomic bomb just three years before and felt embittered toward Americans. Nevertheless, he consented to show the two women around his store and was intrigued when Keller picked up a special old Imari pot. As she examined it with her hands she exclaimed, "Oh, how lovely." Eguchi indignantly thought to himself, "How can this old blind American lady understand the beauty and value of this pot!"

Seven years later, Helen Keller and Anne Sullivan made a second trip to Nagasaki and again visited the pottery store. Imagine Eguchi's surprise when Keller asked him to show her the Imari pot she had "seen" years before. On hearing this, Eguchi realized he had previously misjudged Helen Keller's capacity for appreciation. He would later

write of this episode, "It is not by our eyes that we appreciate pottery. It is our hearts that feel the beauty of pottery."

Perhaps Eguchi lived long enough to realize that it is our hearts that feel the beauty of everything.

gratitude

"If the only prayer you say in your whole life is 'thank you,' that would suffice."

—MEISTER ECKHART

Gratitude is a precursor to delight. To be truly happy is to live in gratitude. In awakened awareness, we feel grateful simply for life itself. That we exist at all, witnessing the wonders of life for the span of our existence, is an immeasurable gift and reason enough to live entirely in gratitude. Yet, as our awareness deepens and expands, we find gratitude for all kinds of things, great and small, happy and sad, within that existence.

In Dharma Dialogues, people often ask me about the meaning of grace. I reply that grace is gratitude. In fact, the words "grace" and "gratitude" share the same Latin root. Living in grace means accepting whatever comes one's way with thankfulness. Grace is not, as is commonly misunderstood, a situation whereby everything goes your way. People will mistakenly think that they were in some sort of grace because they were bumped into first class or chanced to meet the right person at the right time or any other such lucky occurrence. But true grace is an attitude of acceptance and appreciation for whatever comes our way, the hardships as well as the joys. Grace is the openheartedness that whispers "okay" while everything is falling apart.

There is a story of an old wise woman named Suko who lived in Japan and was known for her great joy. One day a man came to visit her and said, "I am very self-centered and unhappy most of the time. Please tell me how to become joyous." Suko replied, "Whatever happens to you, simply say to the universe, 'Thank you; thank you for everything. I have no complaints whatsoever.'" She told him to come back in a year and report to her his progress.

The man left and one year later returned to Suko. He reported that he had been doing what she had told him. He had been saying "thank you" for everything. But, alas, he was still self-absorbed and miserable. "Now what?" he asked.

And Suko said, "Again say, 'Thank you. Thank you for all of it. I have no complaints whatsoever.'" It is said that the man realized in that moment the true power of gratitude, that there was no exception to what one can be thankful for, and that even his misery could be seen with appreciation. It had worn down his resistance, humbled him, and brought him to the wise woman. As the story goes, he entered into a stream of everlasting joy.

Some years ago when I was living in Portland, Oregon, the writer Andrew Harvey came to visit me when he was in town to lead a workshop. Upon his arrival on an unusually hot summer day, we went to the famous Japanese Gardens of Portland and then drove into town to do some errands. Errands completed, we walked back to where I thought we had parked the car, but the car was nowhere to be found. As we searched block after block, my mind raced to the possibility that the car had been stolen, as I knew that this particular area of town had a high rate of car theft.

Onward we paced in the midday heat. After nearly an hour I noticed that Andrew, who had a bad back, was beginning to move a lot more slowly. Tentatively, I asked him what was in his luggage that had been left in the car. "Well . . . my passport, the notes to my new manuscript, and seven hundred dollars in cash," he said. "But you have lost your whole car," he added sympathetically.

As we walked, Andrew remarked on the beautiful architecture of the buildings we were passing. He noted that, given the propensity for rain in Portland, we were lucky to be dry in our current endeavor. He stopped to admire a small vegetable garden in a front yard. Each time he spoke, it was to appreciate something of beauty. Soon, I found my own resistance to the lost car situation melting away. If the car was stolen, it was already gone. We would file the police reports and find a way home. There was no point in missing the lovely architecture and gardens along our way. So after a while, I too began to notice little aspects of sweet life that passed before me on that summer day: the smells from the street food vendors, an old lady smiling in a wheelchair with face turned to the sun, a boy unwrapping a newly purchased kite. We walked in a state of grace, in gratitude.

Eventually we found the car where I had evidently parked and mindlessly left it hours before. Although finding the car was a great relief, the time spent searching for it had been somehow delightful. Wherever there is real appreciation, delight is not far away. The attitude of gratitude is in itself one of the most valued components for delight. This attitude does not depend on the objects for which we are grateful; it is entirely subjective, a way of perceiving, a lens through which we view the world. The lens of gratitude.

A few years ago my brother Glenn became extremely ill and was subsequently diagnosed with AIDS. Having spent his life seeking things outside of himself and in the future for happiness, he had been unhappy for his previous thirty-two years. The diagnosis of AIDS and the prospect of having a shortened life forced his awareness into a deep appreciation of what time and experience is left to him. He is now happier than ever before. He would not say he is grateful for having AIDS. But having AIDS has made him grateful for life.

If we could know the day and hour of our death, we might well experience an appreciation for every breath, sight, sound, or touch. And though most of us do not know the exact hour of our death, we can be sure that it will come soon enough. Perhaps at the juncture between being and being no more, we will appreciate the gift of life, but why wait until the end to do so? The gift is no less precious now. Why not let our intelligence be wide awake in gratitude and thereby find delight in each day of this priceless existence?

a contagion of joy

"Let joy be unconfined."

—LORD BYRON

For nearly a year while living in the San Francisco Bay area, I would go from my home in Marin County into the city of San Francisco across the Golden Gate Bridge in the late afternoon. There was in those days a toll taker, an older black man of infectious delight, who seemed to me an embodiment of awakened awareness. In the few seconds it took to hand him the toll or for him to return change, he always offered a sweet word and a smile. I found myself making sure to get in his lane as I approached the tollbooth, and after a while it felt like visiting an old friend. No matter the weather or the amount of traffic on the bridge, he was impervious to gloom. "What a beautiful day," he would beam. "So nice to see you."

I noticed on quite a number of occasions that if the car ahead of me had children in it, the toll taker would hand something to each of them. One day when there was no one waiting behind me, I asked him what it was that he gave to the children. "Oh, that's from my stash of Tootsie Rolls," he said, showing me a jumbo bag of the candies. "I like to give the little ones a treat because some of them are on long road trips."

Once, while sitting in traffic on the bridge, I tried to mentally calculate the number of people with whom the toll taker might come into contact in an eight-hour shift. I tried to imagine how many people his friendliness might be affecting, if only a small fraction of them were responsive to it. I don't remember the number of my estimate now, only that it seemed significantly high. I know that in my own case, those few moments of meeting him each day were a reminder of joy, and I marveled at how much delight this one man, in an unenviable job, was potentially spreading around. "This guy should work at the U.N.," I thought to myself.

Our happiness is a gift not only to ourselves but to everyone in our lives. Whether we are exuberant in our expressions or merely twinkling in silence, joy can be contagious for those around us. Most of us know the experience of laughter starting up in perhaps an inappropriate context and being impossible to contain. Soon no one remembers or cares what started it, but the whole thing has become too hilarious to stop. In this same way, a current of joy can spread from a particular person and after a while those around him or her cannot remember its origins, only that they are feeling helplessly delighted.

Our happiness also gives the gift of a lack of worry about us to our loved ones. They can cross us off their list of anxieties. In fact, when loved ones think of us in their own moments of difficulty, it soothes and reminds them of well-being, of safe harbor. A beam of light rushing into a cavern of darkness.

Many years ago while forming a service organization that dealt with numerous international tragedies, I became agitated and depressed. The truth was that, as laudable as the organization was, I didn't like the work and brought little joy to it. I was there because I thought I should be, and at least some of my motivation concerned the way my being involved with such an important project looked to others. One day, my friend Howie Cohn came to have lunch with me. He had just returned from a trip to India in which he had met the man who would eventually become my own teacher, Poonjaji. As we walked to the restaurant, I could feel the heaviness of each of my steps in comparison to

Howie's lightness of foot and heart. He talked very little of his time with Poonjaji, but a warmth of joy poured from his every move and word. His mind was clear, refreshing, and playful. I found myself laughing deeply for the first time in weeks.

When I returned to the office, I knew I had to leave that job (and soon thereafter did). If we are not bringing joy to a circumstance, our service is questionable. We may be trudging on like good soldiers, but it is not inspiring. When we are awake in delight, our very presence is encouraging. Even the thought of us is helpful to someone in difficulty. In times of unhappiness I often envision the face of the Dalai Lama and am immediately reminded that there is a possibility of joy in the most trying of situations. The Dalai Lama consistently radiates happiness even though he is daily aware of enormous suffering in Tibet and elsewhere. This is, of course, not to deny sadness. It is simply to know the channel of delight that prevails in awakened awareness; it prevails in sadness as well.

Years ago, a man whose girlfriend had just been murdered attended one of our retreats. Understandably, this man had enormous sadness coursing through him, along with a general numbness to the world. We held his suffering in our hearts in a gentle sharing of that horrific loss, an amortizing of the burden. Yet so strong was the power of being with others in retreat that after a few days he was able to feel himself, to cry, and to begin to appreciate the beauty that surrounded him. He even managed to experience delight; several times during the group sessions I noticed him heartily laughing as day by day he brightened in the contagion of love and joy that surrounded him. And although he may well have dipped again into grief upon leaving the comfort of the loving retreat community, he had at least been reminded of the well of happiness still possible, despite the terrible loss he had suffered.

Delight is the natural antidote to misery. In awakened awareness we let our delight shine just a little brighter in the company of others in case anyone else's lantern of joy has dimmed. And just as with the lighting of one lantern from another, there is only a surge of brightness in the combined illumination, with no diminishment of light to the original lantern. A gift that renews and enhances itself merely by giving.

the moon is always full

"Be in love with your life."

—JACK KEROUAC, *LIST OF ESSENTIALS*

Throughout each month we refer to the moon in its various stages according to our view of it. We call it a sliver moon, a quarter moon, a half moon, or a full moon. The moon, in its wholeness, might be surprised by how many billions of people have seen it as otherwise, since the moon, unto itself, is always full.

Just so, in awakened awareness, we know we are whole in ourselves, no matter what anyone else's perception of us might be. Our lives and experiences are uniquely our own, tapestries whose every thread is in its place, even as they continue to be woven. No one else can fully know the quivers of inspiration or tender silent observations that comprise our mental landscape. We revel in them mostly without articulation or need for acknowledgment. It is a secret delight.

For much of my adult life I had the notion that surrounding myself with exciting people and having exotic adventures around the world would enhance my person. It seemed, too, that having these kinds of experiences and people in my life would induce admiration from others. I would be an enchanting person in their eyes and, without any conscious decision about this, I felt I would be a deeper and happier person in myself. Wanderlust and an appetite for experiences that seemed edgy, radical, or even dangerous prompted me to keep on the move, relentlessly notching new places, ideas, amazing characters, and all kinds of mind experimentation onto the belt of "me." I became, in my mind, a collection of intriguing adventure stories and a hub for fascinating people.

In this pursuit I also felt that the lives of people in more simple, stay-at-home existences were small and stifling. Oh, there were the exceptions, of course. Emily Dickinson stayed put in her home in Massachusetts and wrote great poetry. Shakespeare probably didn't get around much but intellectually changed the world. These and other gifted people managed to have extraordinary interior lives without a lot of travel or the company of exciting society. But secretly, I thought that most people who were living quiet simple lives, perhaps raising a family, working a job until retirement, or farming some land, were generally boring and likely narrow-minded.

Of course, time has a way of humbling us and forcing us to reconsider long held opinions. It became clear that, despite my dedication to the glamorous bohemian life, the addition of experiences did not necessarily induce a deepening of quality, insight, or happiness. It also became clear that the so-called ordinary life of most people was not necessarily limited in quality, insight, or happiness by the fact that they didn't travel much or have sophisticated friends. In other words, the delights and profundity of any life depend on the internal relationship we have with our own wholeness and not on the external accumulation of experiences and people.

Leo Tolstoy told a story about three Christian hermits living for decades on an island near northern Russia. Learning of their reputation for holiness and asceticism, a bishop decided to pay them a visit and to teach them what he could. Upon his arrival on the island, the bishop said, "Tell me, how do you pray to God?"

"We pray in this way," replied the hermits. "Three are ye, three are we, have mercy on us!"

Smiling, the bishop recognized their misguided attempt to honor the Holy Trinity but patiently explained to the hermits that they did not pray correctly. For many hours he expounded on faith and taught the hermits traditional prayers, making them repeat phrases a hundred times over. Taking leave of them, the bishop thanked God for having sent him to help such worthy but confused men. Back on the ship that night the bishop could not sleep, so excited was he by his accomplishment with the hermits. After several hours had passed, however, he noticed something bright and shining, moving on the moonlit sea. As the vision came more into focus, he plainly saw that it was the three hermits running across the top of the water at a fantastic speed.

"We have forgotten your teaching, Servant of God," announced the hermits as they approached the boat. "As long as we kept repeating it we remembered, but when we stopped for a while, it went all to pieces. Please teach us again."

Stunned by what he had just witnessed, the bishop bowed low before them and said, "Your own prayer will reach the Lord, men of God. It is not for me to teach you."

Living in wholeness gives each of our lives power and dignity, no matter the apparent limitations of our circumstances, knowledge, or life experiences. Accepting life without second-guessing how it should have been or might be allows us to truly enjoy life as it is. Recently I saw a documentary about some Hispanic ghetto kids in a school in Los Angeles. The film particularly focused on a young, slightly overweight girl named Mayra who appeared to be about nine or ten years old. Very bright and talkative in fluent English, Mayra revealed her innermost self in a way rarely seen among young people, and each word she said made her more endearing.

I was especially struck by Mayra's joy as she proudly showed the filmmaker around the one-room tenement in East Los Angeles that she shared with her sibling, mother, and uncle. With everything neatly in its place, she pointed out where each of the family slept in various bunks, and she meticulously went through the carefully arranged sections of the one and only closet allotted to them, noting which grouping of clothing belonged to which family member. Mayra spends most of her days alone in this room after school while her mother and uncle work at menial jobs to support the family. Yet seeing her clomping around in her mother's high heels and dancing a few steps for the camera, I felt she may as well have been on a stage in front of thousands, so great was the pleasure she seemed to take in the act.

In awakened awareness we no longer demand that the context of our lives provide our happiness, nor do we hope to view our wholeness through anyone else's eyes. Mayra has not yet learned to diminish her experience by telling herself that the circumstances of her life leave much to be desired or that others might feel sorry for her. Her joy is the happiness of one who simply feels fine about herself, a full moon dancing in a tenement.

contentment

"He who binds himself to a joy
Doth the winged life destroy
He who kisses the joy as it flies
Lives in eternity's sunrise."

—WILLIAM BLAKE

Contentment is perhaps the most underrated aspect of happiness in our culture. Mostly we are conditioned by advertising and society to equate contentment with boredom. From an early age we are inducted in the message that happiness means wanting and getting things. About a week after the destruction of the World Trade Center and the loss of nearly three thousand lives, our government and media called upon its citizenry for their help. What they suggested was not to count our blessings, or to realize life's uncertainty and be more kind to one another, or to diminish our dependence on foreign resources. No, according to the government and advertising media, the most important and patriotic act for us in the face of the national tragedy was to purchase products. Spend money. Get back to consuming. Like Manchurian Candidates programmed to shop, we are expected to go along in a nearly robotic buying trance upon which even a large-scale catastrophe should barely impinge.

I don't see an evil conspiracy on the part of the government and corporations. Those organizations are comprised simply of people, just folks. But there are a number of fallacies under which many of the people in those institutions operate. They assume that wanting more and always being hungry for the next thing is a desirable condition. They are engaged in this assumption, not to pull one over on an unsuspecting public, but because they, too, want more things and are trying to get them. They just happen to be in positions of power that allow them to readily do so by convincing masses of people likewise. It's a pyramid scheme on a large scale. Unfortunately, the players are slow to notice that this is not leading to happiness and that the runaway train of consumption is killing much of life on the earth. If we were all more content, we would consume less. Contentment therefore becomes one of the most revolutionary acts a person in Western culture can experience. But feeling content goes against all cultural norms and conditioning, and that is why it is so rare.

In awakened awareness, however, contentment seeps into one's being like the smell of ocean on a tropical breeze. Because one is not distracted by stories of what is missing, one's appreciation of what is here becomes subtler. A former entertainment lawyer and television writer who attends Dharma Dialogues told me recently that he can scarcely believe his ability to watch birds from the window of his apartment and feel completely content. He no longer has a need to be bombarded with media stimuli in order to feel entertained. In fact, he has begun to experience such bombardment as an assault on his senses. His taste has become more refined. Content with simpler things and less interested in elaborate drama, he experiences now a peace he had never known during many years of seeking and acquiring.

Perhaps the greatest example of contentment that I know of is the life of Ramana Maharshi. One of the most revered of contemporary Indian sages, Ramana had an extraordinary awakening in 1896 when he was just sixteen years old. After school one day, young Ramana was overcome by the thought of death. How could it be that everyone was destined to die? More to the point, how could it be that *he* was going to die? Stricken with fear, he lay down and allowed his awareness to examine what exactly it was that would die and what could possibly remain. In the span of twenty minutes he realized what he called the Self, the substratum of existence, which infuses everything. Because he recognized his fundamental nature as that substratum, the fear of death left him and never returned. Moreover, he was filled with love, an appreciation of the Self in all its forms. So absorbed was he in this newfound delight that he could no longer bear the mundane activities of life as a schoolboy. Ordinary studies seemed to him a distraction from his immersion in Self. Six weeks after his realization, he left home and went directly to the mountain Aruna-chala, a sacred pilgrimage spot that had always held a mysterious lure for him.

There, on and around the mountain, Ramana spent the rest of his life. So great was his contentment that until his death in 1950 he never left Arunachala, even for a day. For many of his initial years there he lived in complete silence, dwelling in caves, clad only in a loincloth. After some time, devotees began to collect around him, drawn by the silent love that emanated from him. Eventually, an ashram formed to accommodate the devotees and visitors. Scholars, writers, heads of state, spiritual teachers, and seekers from around the world also came to sit in his presence. Over the years, Ramana would occasionally answer questions but mostly he remained silent, helping out with ashram chores, tending to the animals, or resting on his dais. Having never sought the world, the world came to him.

I was a young woman when I first saw a photo of Ra-mana Maharshi, taken in his later years. I remember looking at the picture and having the thought, "That is what I would like to look like at that age." His face radiated contentment; his eyes gazed into forever. It was perhaps the most beautiful face I had ever seen. I attempted to read a few of his teachings, but they were too simple and direct for my complicated spiritual needs and beliefs at the time. It was a long journey to come home to them. Who could have known that in meeting Poonjaji nearly twenty years later I would find myself with a teacher whose own living teacher had been Ramana Maharshi?

The deepest contentment comes from recognizing the pervading life force in everything. It is the experience of witnessing an infinitely creative intelligence endlessly manifesting itself. We call its comings and goings *life* and *death*. But from another perspective, all is consciousness, endlessly rearranging itself into form and formlessness. There is no need to demand that its creatures of form should continue past death in some manner when the underlying reality from which they spring is infinite. Knowing this, we are witnesses to eternity, if only for a very short while.

wonder

The sun was setting as the moon rose. They were now in the sky together; the sun lit in gold, the moon in pearl. She knew that both glowed from the same light, and she wondered where this light originated. What, in fact, was light? She pondered the question of light only briefly, and then her mind fell into silence.

Next came reflections on existence itself. Why was there anything at all? This question, too, disappeared into space. Similar thoughts about the origins and destination of things continued to arise and vanish without resolution, leaving her in a pleasant feeling of wonder. She basked in how little she knew, the burden of wanting to know having released itself with the end of the quest.

Strange, she once thought that it was possible to unravel the mysteries of life. She had studied various traditions of knowledge and philosophy and had aligned her mind with those that most appealed. They represented vast and ancient systems of training and dedication, with texts filling thousands of libraries. She had assumed that at least one of these traditions had to be right. But that was in the time of the quest. Now she had no such assumptions. She had moved from the conjecture of knowing to the certainty of not knowing.

She remembered similar feelings from childhood. She had lived in a grand mystery back then. Though excited by the endless possibilities of existence, she had spent little time actually thinking about them. Her days as a child were too rich and wonderful to spend pondering things she could not know.

Now she had come back to a sense of wonder, once again walking in a mysterious universe, feeling like a child. She didn't know the origins of her existence or what might come next. She had no books to which she could refer for answers, no traditions in which to find company, no beliefs to promise anything more than this moment. Yet she had never been more content. She was a lover of mystery, after all, and mystery surrounded her.

The sun had set. Shades of twilight and moonlight painted the sky and landed on the river in great ribbons of purple and silver. She silently watched the dazzling play of colors on the water, her own eyes reflecting their mysterious light.

what is all this?

> *"Our situation on this earth seems strange. Every one of us appears here involuntarily and uninvited, for a short stay, without knowing why. To me it is enough to wonder at the secrets."*
>
> —ALBERT EINSTEIN

A friend of mine bought a telescope for his eight-year-old daughter, and on a full-moon night they set it up in the backyard. He fixed the lens on the moon so that it took up the entire view and then had his daughter take a look. Astonished at the sight, his daughter said, "Look, Dad, the moon is moving." Her father explained to her that the moon was indeed moving around the earth, just as the earth was moving around the sun. In a moment of revelation, the wide-eyed girl exclaimed, "Oh my god, we're in space!"

Almost everyone has at some time or other known those wondrous moments when suddenly no boundaries limit the felt sense of existence. In awakened awareness this feeling becomes normalized. It is simply the truth of the matter. As my teacher once put it, "This very *now,* can you measure its breadth, its height, its depth?" The question delivers the mind into vastness.

Awakened awareness is awestruck by the mystery of life. We might be delighted by new revelations about our world, but we are also happy to humbly know that we don't know much. It takes an honest heart and mind to acknowledge that we don't really know what purpose there is to existence or that there is any purpose at all. The concept of purpose may be merely a human conceit.

Being content with the mystery is somewhat rare, it seems, as most people want answers and console themselves with belief systems about the origins of the cosmos. They want the known, no matter how irrational. But anyone who has been rendered speechless in the presence of beauty, genius, love, birth, or death, anyone who simply observes the most mundane of this fantastic existence and marvels at the stunning intelligence that informs it, lives in a sense of aliveness that no religion or belief can provide.

In our retreats, the feeling of wonder becomes stronger by the day. This is due to the power of observation that comes when we are quiet and the free flow of natural intelligence is allowed to reign. We question what we were once sure we knew, and we then perceive with the clarity of seeing as if for the first time. One of our retreat participants once joked in a morning session: "I looked in the mirror and didn't recognize the face, but I shaved it anyway." He didn't recognize his own face because the stories associated with his face, his this-is-who-I-am habits, were simply not there.

Since childhood I have had similar experiences with the face in the mirror. I remember passing mirrors as a young girl and stopping, suddenly stunned and curious about the creature whose reflection I saw there. I would look at my image with an intense but impersonal interest as though I had rounded a corner and come face to face with my clone. I recall in those memories not only the sense of "What is that?" but, as the awareness bolted from its usual confines, the larger sense of "What is all of this?"

Given the preciousness of existence and our short time here, how does our awareness lose its natural sense of wonder? How do we become dulled into a metronomic life of just moving forward, checking off to-do lists, competing as needed, buying on cue? What inhibits our natural intelligence from the full appreciation of living in a grand mystery? Two primary culprits are fear and cynicism.

Fear, of course, can be learned and cultivated. Children who are indoctrinated in various religious beliefs from a young age grow up with terrifying pictures of what happens if they don't believe the version of reality offered by their particular religion. They are told they will burn in hell forever, for example. Not only is it unfairly easy to indoctrinate a child, but with an added inducement of eternal damnation if the doctrine is even questioned, it is really a wonder that anyone ever dares. Children who don't dare question grow up in the acceptance of this fear and try to conform to their religion's version of good behavior, an attempt at which many people fail.

One of my friends who grew up as a Catholic told me that he first kissed a girl at the age of fourteen. He said that the moment their lips touched he knew that he would have to resign himself to hell because there was no way he would be able to resist kissing again at every opportunity. He lived with guilt for years, but eventually he began to question the entire dogma on which his fear and suppression of natural instincts was based. He was one of the brave ones; he broke loose and has been soaring ever since. Many are not so lucky, and their spirits sink into listlessness and resignation. It reminds me of zoo animals whose nature demands that they roam across the Serengeti but whose circumstances confine them to an eight-by-eight-foot cage. In this same way, the nature of one who is confined in fear within a belief system, who has lost all sense of wonder, dims and twists in on itself. It is a breeding ground for misery as well as for miserable actions, as we can plainly see in the reign of terror by repressed religious fundamentalists currently under way.

Fear can also develop without the conditioning of beliefs imposed by others. Many people grow up in liberal and secular households and still end up in belief systems that have no supporting evidence whatsoever. This is due to the powerful human resistance to the unknown. This resistance may even be genetically predisposed, an aspect of evolution that favors planning. Humans naturally want to know what lies ahead and have a fear of being out of control if they don't. But again, the reliance on beliefs out of fear of the unknown limits our sense of wonder and diminishes our lives.

Cynicism is also based on beliefs, though they take a different form from those of fear. It nevertheless has the same effect of dimming the light of life. The particular ennui of cynicism is sometimes said to be simply the disappointment of a former idealism. Perhaps having once embraced traditional or exotic beliefs and found them wanting, the one-time idealist becomes a cynic, unfortunately bypassing the realm of wonder.

The cynical view proposes that the laws governing life are totally mechanistic and indifferent at best, randomly cruel at worst. These are conclusions based on only partial evidence that overlooks the abundant displays of love, mercy, beauty, intelligence, and kindness that comprise life as well. Cynical conclusions also assume facts not in evidence, proposing that existence is merely some elements emerging from gas and dust and now pointlessly banging around in space. Yes, we came from gas and dust, but the cynical conclusion neglects to fully consider the intelligence that is informing existence, of which our own intelligence must be a tiny microcosm. We haven't understood even this earthly intelligence or consciousness so near at hand. It therefore seems premature to assume anything about the purpose or lack thereof of the universal intelligence.

The religious and New Age believers, in their convictions and fantasies, don't really know the secrets of existence, but neither do the cynics in their assumptions of mechanistic purposelessness. Both groups would benefit by releasing their imagined certainty and thereby opening the floodgates to wonder. In awakened awareness, there is a natural vigilance with regard to both hope and cynicism, an intelligence that notices the discomfort of relying on a belief that cannot be verified or, in some fit of unhappiness, concluding that existence means nothing at all. The preferred experience—and the truest—is that of the mysterious.

What is all this? In awakened awareness, there is no need for answers to the questions of existence. We are content to live with the questions, and sometimes find that they, too, fall away. All that remains is wonder. It is a return to innocence and at the same time a maturity of spirit. Wide-eyed and wise. At home with nowhere to stand. This quality keeps a freshness to the intelligence that is not in the furrowed brow of the questioner who needs to know, but in the face of the child gazing at the night sky.

fascination

During an evening of Dharma Dialogues years ago, an engineer spoke of an issue that was troubling him. He said that he spent time pondering too many things, particularly about how things worked. He felt this intense curiosity indicated a mind that could not be quiet, a mind that needed distraction. By example, he described his interest in how the electrical fixtures were hung in the room in which we sat, and as he did so his eyes gleamed with excitement. Yet he felt embarrassed for being so fascinated with the material world. He thought his fascination with the workings of things meant he wasn't a spiritual kind of guy.

The engineer's assumptions about curiosity are not as unfounded as they might seem. There are many spiritual schools and traditions that eschew interest in the world. They would have us believe that our world is merely a snare of illusion and that fascination in anything about it indicates a deluded mind. As I mentioned in an earlier chapter, these notions abound in traditions of pure transcendence, which imagine some higher realm and view this world's attractions as pitfalls to avoid.

But it is a great misconception to think that the spiritual life requires a receding curiosity about our world. Although there are cases, such as that of Ramana Maharshi, in which interest in the manifest world diminishes and turns instead to an intense absorption in silence, this is not necessarily how it is for everyone who lives in wakefulness. Our wonder and fascination, like everything about ourselves, is unique to each of us.

And strange indeed are our fascinations. Prior to his publication of *The Origin of Species,* Charles Darwin spent nearly a decade in the study of barnacles. His estate became a barnacle repository as collectors from around the world sent him specimens. Darwin's fascination was evidently so much a part of his home life that his young son, after visiting a neighbor's house, innocently inquired, "But where does he do his barnacles?" It might have been a revelatory moment for the child to discover that not all men are fascinated with barnacles.

We may be equally fascinated by what we can know in form and what we can sense in formlessness. The Dalai Lama, though dedicated to a lifelong study of meditation and dharma, has always loved to know the workings of mechanical things. Although he was recognized as the political and spiritual leader of Tibet at the age of four and was therefore the most privileged young man in his country, he liked nothing better than to repair things. At the Norbulingka palace, where the Dalai Lama spent his summers as a child, there was an unreliable old generator used for electric light. It provided ample excuse for the young spiritual leader to "take it to pieces" and thereby learn how internal combustion engines work. Later he would work on a movie projector and then several automobiles, which had been carried in parts over the Himalayas and into his hidden land. His fascination with the workings of things has gone on for decades. In a documentary called *Compassion in Exile,* he is seen taking apart watches in order to put them together again while cheerfully explaining that it is his way of relaxing.

A fascination for Einstein revolved around something that we take for granted but don't actually understand. "For the rest of my life," he said, "I want to reflect on what light is."

Who knows what will turn us on? Whatever it may be, when we are soaring in wonder we are connected to the divine. In awakened awareness, we trust our fascination to be an aspect of existence wanting to know itself through another aspect of existence, like facets of a jewel, each intrigued by the other's color. When our attention is not wearied by neurosis, it is free to hover around whatever strikes its fancy, be it barnacles or silent immersion in being. One's awareness mingles with its object of interest, and there is that wonderful feeling of forgetting oneself that is actually a remembered aliveness. This is what is meant when we say we are lost in something we love. "She was lost in painting for hours." "He was lost in his woodworking project." "They were lost in each other's eyes." The direct experience is actually that we are whole and fully present, not lost but found. We are not obsessing about our small sense of self, so it is only the constricted sense of *I* that is "lost." What is found is a greater sense of being.

A mind released from self-obsession and limiting beliefs is freed for fascination, for wonder, for love. In fact, in awakened awareness fascination is a form of love, a desire to experience oneself more fully in the limitless exploration of "other." Our awareness is forced to enlarge itself to accommodate the new, and widening the awareness in this way is exhilarating, like removing a tight suit and slipping into pajamas or into the arms of your lover.

I have often wondered why people the world over love movies. Film and television have become the most compelling entertainment media in the world; the desire for movies and drama crosses all cultures. Of course, drama in theater and playacting of various forms goes back many centuries. Why are we so fascinated with seeing stories acted out? In my own case, it is for the experience of condensed life. After being swept away by a film, I leave the theater feeling as though I have just lived several lives completely different from that of my own. My awareness has entered their reality and assimilated it. Watching films, experiencing life compressed into short visual stories, becomes an ongoing merger with manifestation, an education that reveals the one in the many, the many in the one. We *feel* what it is like to be one of the others, to care about his problems or to exalt in her joys. We (most of us) root for the good guys to win, but in drama we also applaud the villain, especially when he is convincing in his role. He, too, is included in our expanded scope of what we are, and he forces us to feel his torment.

Finally it is this love of feeling that drives fascination— feeling ourselves anew, enlarged by understanding and empathy, enlivened by curiosity. In awakened awareness there is no shunning of fascination. It is a welcomed aspect of passion, a way to know that we are fully alive.

the spirit of adventure

"The real voyage of discovery consists not in seeking new landscapes, but in having new eyes."

—MARCEL PROUST

Awakened awareness is sometimes likened to being swept into a wave of universal intelligence. You are standing on the riverbank of conditioned mind and belief, clutching a branch of dogma, hoping to stay put, and suddenly a torrent of white water rushes by and sweeps you off your feet. Nothing to do but surrender and enjoy the rapids. Like this, one's conditioned mind is out of the way and what roars through is the intelligence of the creative force of existence. Suddenly, one is interested in the process. Moving from dogma to the unknown is also a movement from dullness to aliveness, and life becomes an exploration, a celebration.

Adventure is an impulse born of wonder. Although most people tend to equate adventure with travel, actually adventure can occur in both motion and stillness. One's body may be stationary and yet there may be an incredible journey taking place in a cascade of insight. It is not necessary to cover a lot of ground. Some of my greatest adventures have occurred in a small amount of space, in either silence or in intimacy with another.

Much of what calls us to adventure is the urge to experience ourselves in fresh ways. We want to feel that wonderful expansion that comes when we merge with something new and different. It is not the thing in itself—the new city, museum, deserted beach, temple, gondola ride, mountain— it is who we are in the new experience that calls us to the journey. The main adventure is within ourselves. It is the spirit, our inner sense of being, that has the real adventure. We keep surprising ourselves, discovering anew the mystery of who we are when we blend with an entirely new circumstance.

In 1977, I visited the region of Ladakh in India with my oldest friend, Alan Clements. We rocked and bumped on a two-day bus ride from Srinagar, Kashmir, along the world's scariest washed-out road and into the high desert of the Himalayas, the bus wheels often only inches from unprotected cliff edges of mile-long descents. Every now and again all passengers would be required to disembark from the bus in order to clear the road of rocks from a recent avalanche. And every now and again we would see the stone markers of a memorial for passengers of a bus that had plunged over the side.

Ladakh, perched on the outer regions of the Tibetan plateau, was at that time probably more like old Tibet than contemporary Tibet, which was (and is today) under the restriction of Chinese rule. The Ladakh plateau rises as a moonscape of mostly desert and rocks. At an average altitude of over eleven thousand feet, the air is thin and the colors of the sky and mountains particularly vivid.

Virtually no other tourists came to Ladakh in those days, and consequently there were few accommodations for visitors. We found a room in the upstairs of a Ladakhi family's house in Leh, the capital, and were allotted a pail of a shockingly small amount of water per day, enough only to brush our teeth and wash our faces. We would have to find our drinking and bathing water in the market and pay dearly for it.

Clad in colorful traditional dress and jewelry of turquoise and coral, people with mountain faces milled about in the market in their daily business and prayers, almost all of them readily smiling when one happened to catch their eye. With the exception of a few young boys, each offering to be our "guide," almost no one spoke English.

There were no cars, no radios, no televisions. Occasionally, distant sounds of strange horns and wood flutes punctuated the relative quiet.

Visiting Ladakh was a pilgrimage for us, a way of paying homage to an ancient Buddhist culture. As practicing Buddhists at the time, we hoped to visit some of the temples and to immerse ourselves in the daily life of the people. For several months we had planned the trip while in the plains of India and had made the long journey north with Kipling-esqe dreams of what Ladakh might be. Although we had both traveled to other exotic lands, we knew that we had probably never seen anything quite like Ladakh.

We had been warned that the only other "foreigners" in the area were the Indian army and its officers, who kept a strong show of force in Ladakh due to its close proximity to the border of Pakistan. It seemed a shame, I remember thinking, that this beautiful unspoiled place was sullied by a large military presence.

One day we were in the market when an impeccably dressed Indian army officer in a dark blue Sikh turban said hello to us. We politely said hello and went on our way. The next day we bumped into the same officer again. This time we had a brief conversation. I had the sense that the officer was a little lonely for company other than fellow army officers. He told us that none of their families were with them on this assignment.

The third time we ran into him, the officer invited us to

dinner at the general's compound that evening. Having nothing else to do at night (and I mean nothing!) and thinking there was a good chance of getting some decent food, we accepted. It was the beginning of a bizarre chapter of our journey. For the next couple weeks we spent our evenings with the Indian army elite in Ladakh, becoming friends with the general and senior officers. We ate imported delicacies, drank wine, played cards, stayed out till midnight, and were chauffeured home by army drivers. In fact, when it was eventually time to go, the general sent us all the way back to Kashmir in his jeep.

The more we learned of our hosts, the more fascinating they seemed to us. Because Ladakh was considered a potential hot spot, the Indian army selected some of their most gifted officers for the post. Almost all were educated in England's finest universities, fluent in several languages, and internationally savvy. Our nights flew by in stimulating geopolitical conversations as well as in discussions on spirituality, art, and science.

On our first few visits with the army officers I felt a disturbing low-level guilt. We had come all this way to experience the fascinating culture of Ladakh. What were we doing indulging in Western-style comforts (which seemed a little obscene in this setting) and hanging out with the military, for god's sake? We were serious dharma practitioners, seekers who lived outside conventional norms and were opposed to military organizations on principle. Why were we wasting our time in a circumstance so clearly not connected to our true path? Each night when we would leave the compound I doubted that we would return the next night, but the next night would roll around and there we would be. I felt disoriented about who I was and what I stood for, as though I was slipping into an underworld.

After some days, my awareness acclimated and expanded to include the new circumstance. I had to proceed purely on instincts and love. We had made friends with these people. They were kind and generous to us and didn't seem to have any particular bloodlust for fighting. They were men doing their jobs in a faraway outpost, making the best of being away from their families, and dedicated to protecting their country, an endeavor that, with time, I have grown to appreciate. Due to our shared language, these were the only people in the region with whom we had developed a bond. My heart opened and let them in, and there they live to this day. When I think of my time in Ladakh, it is the faces of those army officers that I see. Yes, we had traveled to a land that was remote in both space and time, and we had many adventures along the way. But from that experience I learned, yet again, that the true adventure takes place in the heart.

creation's mirror

*"It is merely the Immaculate
Looking naturally at itself."*

—NYOSHUL KHENPO RINPOCHE

According to modern astronomy, our solar system was formed some four and a half billion years ago when a cloud of interstellar gas and dust condensed into itself, forming a broad and rather flat disk. At its dense center there formed the sun, a blazing ball of thermonuclear fire around which swirled millions of rocky chunks, some of which would merge together to form planets. This process apparently repeats itself throughout the universe. In 1994, the Hubble Space Telescope sent back dazzling images of new stars similarly forming in the constellation Orion. In the observable universe alone it is estimated that about one hundred such solar systems are forming every second.

Today the planets along with other large space matter swirl around the fiery center in our solar system on the same flat plane as they did at the time of their formation. What has dramatically changed, however, is the phenomenal variety of life that has sprung up on the third planet from the sun, our Earth. Apparently abundant in conditions for life, Earth sits strategically not too far from or too close to the sun. It is protected for the most part from devastating collisions with intergalactic space debris by our massive neighbor planet Jupiter, which has so far taken the largest hits for us.

In the early days, organic matter was generated by sunlight on earth or fell to earth from space, becoming the building blocks for primitive life nearly four billion years ago. The first known life forms are called stromatolites, which are large collections of layered bacteria, dating to three and a half billion years ago. It is assumed, however, that stromatolites had much more primitive ancestors of one-celled organisms or small molecular systems, but the fossil record does not go back that far due to the earth's ancient crust having been subsumed far into its core.

From these humble beginnings life emerged in a fantastic surge of creativity. Over the next few billion years and despite many catastrophic eradications, living things persisted in the oceans and eventually on land. Adaptations of stunning variety morphed and replaced previous designs. Life forms came and went. The current estimate of thirty million species on earth represents probably only 1 percent of all the species that have ever lived. Of the living species, a relative newcomer known as Homo sapiens arrived on the scene about a hundred thousand years ago and evolved to become the most dominant and self-reflective life form of all. From gas and dust through a remarkable evolutionary journey in the sea and on land, life emerged eventually into a creature who would wonder, "Who am I, and where do I come from?" The late astronomer Carl Sagan described this process as a star's way of looking at itself.

Self-reflection, for all its benefits, comes at a high cost. As humans, we are ever aware of our mortality and of our general vulnerability while alive. We are delicate creatures, as mammals go, and we have compensated with cleverness and an extraordinary ability to adapt to or to change our environments. Nevertheless, the shadow of death hangs like a pall over our every activity, our every tender moment.

Cave drawings and artifacts indicate that when self-reflection and awareness of mortality emerged in evolutionary development, humans the world over developed myths and stories of an afterlife. It is understandable that myths and hopes of an afterlife would be needed to assuage the fear and anxiety of primitive man. It may have even been an evolutionary necessity for man to devote himself to those beliefs in the face of a short dangerous life that included the possibility of being eaten alive. Myths must have helped lessen the fear and provided purpose and a sense of belonging, a knowing of one's place in the world. This worked well enough when there were few people on earth and one would rarely bump into someone who had an entirely different idea about the meaning of life or what happens after death. But then humans began to multiply and became mobile enough to collide with other communities. People began to kill each other over their beliefs, and they have been doing so ever since.

Is it possible that the evolutionary journey could now lead us to a condition of wonder as a replacement for myth? Could our acceptance of death be based in the immediacy of our connection with life? In awakened awareness we directly experience the breath of existence without knowing its origin or destination. This suffices for a feeling of belonging because we sense that it permeates everything else. It also provides an understanding of *impersonal* continuation, not a continuation of the personal *me* but of the fundamental essence from which I emerged and which suffuses my every cell.

Many of the ideas in modern science correspond with these feelings, which explains why so many scientists are mystically inclined. Paradoxically, the more we comprehend of nature, the greater is the mystery of whatever intelligence informs it. Science is therefore not a departure from the mystical; it is ultimately an embrace of it. Science is a threat to religion, not to mysticism. Scientific discoveries continually disprove many religious beliefs while at the same time revealing the existence of an intelligence that pervades everything, the recognition of which coincides exactly with the mystical experience.

When scientists or mystics look deeply into what seems to be emptiness or space, what they find is some kind of presence. Quantum physics now tells us that particles emerge out of so-called emptiness, out of pure space. We can eliminate all particles from a given amount of space,

such that the space is seemingly devoid of anything whatsoever, and suddenly elementary particles will emerge. They
will simply appear out of the void. They are somehow already there *in potentia*. What could possibly be the operat-
ing system that powers this fecund emergence? I once
asked Poonjaji if he thought that love was what powered
creation, and he answered, "I don't even call it love. It is
some kind of fullness, such as the fullness of the ocean
when there are no waves." A burgeoning wholeness merging into itself. And within this wholeness, stardust is looking at itself and wondering, "Who am I?"

*Another dawn. Fog hung on the river as a lone blue heron
glided low over the water, tapping its feet in an approach for a
landing. The bird's colors were almost indistinguishable from
the blue hues of the early morning mist, as though the heron
were merely a movement in camouflage.*

*She watched as the first tendrils of light reached out from the
horizon through gray mist and fog, the sight of them promising
the coming warmth of the sun. She had grown accustomed, in a
remarkably short time, to an intelligence in harmony with its
world. Whatever came her way was welcomed and then set free.
She was alert, yet relaxed. Awake, yet innocent. She moved
through space and it moved through her. All was in its place.*

*Suddenly, she noticed someone standing near the river, the
outline of a woman's shawl becoming clearer in the morning
light. It was the old woman, gazing at the water. She made her*

way to the old one's side and they stood together in silence as the heron took off in a spray of water, first soaring over the river, then into the forest. When they could no longer see the bird, they turned to each other, and, bowing before taking their leave, they went their own ways.

about the author

Catherine Ingram is an internationally known dharma teacher with communities serving several thousand students in the U.S., Europe, and Australia. Since 1992, she has led Dharma Dialogues, which are public events of inquiry into the nature of awakened awareness and its benefits in a life. She also leads numerous silent retreats each year and is founder and president of Living Dharma, an educational non-profit organization dedicated to inquiry and service.

A former journalist specializing in issues of consciousness and activism, Catherine is the author of *In the Foot-steps of Gandhi: Conversations with Spiritual/Social Activists* (Parallax Press, 1990). Since 1982, she has also published approximately 100 articles and served on the editorial staffs of *New Age, East West,* and *Yoga Journal.* She currently lives in Los Angeles.

For information about Catherine's schedule and retreats or to order audio and video tapes of Dharma Dialogues, please visit her Web site at WWW.DHARMADIALOGUES.ORG, or contact the office at:

> Living Dharma
> Box 10431
> Portland, OR 97210
> (503) 246-4235